A Letter to My Prodigal Son

A Letter to My Prodigal Son

∞

Jerry S. Barry

Library of Congress Control Number:		2011901375
ISBN:	Hardcover	978-1-4568-5988-6
	Softcover	978-1-4568-5987-9
	Ebook	978-1-4568-5989-3

This book was printed in the United States of America.

To order additional copies of this book, contact:
Xlibris Corporation
1-888-795-4274
www.Xlibris.com
Orders@Xlibris.com
91293

To my

adopted

foster

daughter

Rachel

Ben

04-14-13

Dedicated to my sons, and all the sons who have adopted me as their father substitute, whoever and wherever they are.

PREFACE

This book was written to communicate directly to growing young men who have little or no access to ideas for guidance such as these. As a youth growing up, I got some of mine in little fragments first from my father, then from extended family members and friends, and finally from books. As a teacher I have encountered youths, boys and girls alike, whom I am convinced have not had even a fragment of guidance, and if they had, it was of the wrong kind. I therefore would like to add my perspective to the other books and voices out there by other persons concerned as I am about the future of our youths. While the contents are directed toward young men, it can easily be adapted to address young women as well. As a father myself of boys and girls from a failed relationship, I certainly can empathize with the circumstances which this book addresses, and trust that it would arouse some curiosity and fervent discussion within the right circles, among the youth themselves.

ACKNOWLEDGMENTS

To God Almighty, whose infinite intelligence I leaned upon, trusting this project was a part of his will.

To my loving wife, Gwen, my greatest fan, who endured my whining for years over the issues contained in this book.

To my friend, and brother of circumstance, Donovan Haughton, with whom over the years I have kneaded and polished these ideas, and who was still able to tolerate me revisiting the same topics again and again.

To my father, Jacob, for being there to be my hero, when I was growing up, and for demonstrating the first of life's lessons I was able to learn.

To my five sons: Ray, Kurt, Ekong, Okera, and Akim, for motivating me to write this book.

To the many children I have taught who looked up to me as their perfect male role model.

To all the single mothers and fathers who shared their experiences and thoughts frankly and sincerely with me.

To all the young men and women everywhere involved in clubs and after-school and volunteer programs in an effort to make a difference.

INTRODUCTION

Oh, my son, you are like all other sons. If I write to you exclusively as my true son, my bias would prevent me from sharing the wisdom I want to share with you because my love and concern for you will get in the way. For so long I have been deprived of the pleasure and satisfaction of being a father, I am afraid that if you were present before me I would not know how to conduct myself. You see, son, I think I understand how reading a letter from me would be just as unbearable as it is for me to write one to you. For you and I would not know where to start. I know it is safer and easier for you to go on pretending that you have or can have a father better than I am, just as other sons can look up to me with admiration to substitute for the dad that has been missing in their lives. You see, I am one among us men today who was fortunate not to be caught in the dragnet for final treatment and branding so that we can all truly be viewed the same. The other sons who seem to adore me are probably still searching to find the qualities for which their minds were trained to look and are relieved so far that they have not found any. That fragile advantage is my glory for being who I really am, merely because I had not graduated from the prison system or held any credentials for crime or civil misconduct. If you were to witness how these fatherless sons dote over me, you will get quite offended and accuse me of misleading them, because of what you know about me. I greatly fear that you may be motivated to lead a crusade against me to chase me off my pedestals, strip me of the medals I had won, and cast me into the pit of disrepute. You are one enemy from whose onslaught I will be unable to escape or protect myself, since you are linked to my senses and still plugged into my heart.

My greatest fear is since you know so much about me, I would hardly be able to defend myself from your attack. As a young child, you had already concluded that I had been cowardly and irresponsible and that whatever good qualities I had left were not deserving of your respect. Your level of reasoning was too sophisticated for my poor intellect. When you were very young, you described me so fluently I hardly recognized myself and swore you had lived in this world before I did and helped to influence my manhood. Often other sons would ask me if I have a son of my own, and I would say yes to avoid disappointing them. They would proceed to ask me questions about you, and I would painfully answer and fill the blanks with lies that would look good on our behalf. As you already know, I have always been a teacher and that my job brings me into contact with youths of all descriptions. There is a common trend, however, in all my meetings and interactions with them: they are all looking for heroes and role models to give shape and structure to their own lives. I suppose that is what you do right now when you encounter your male teachers or your friends' fathers as you speculate how I would compare with these people after the many negative things you have heard. While these youths hunger to absorb as much of my good qualities they could get, you are looking for those same qualities in somebody else, while your environment forces you to focus on the weaker qualities I may have. This is why I am more comfortable socializing with other youths who are not connected to me, because I can be myself and show off my true qualities, even if it is just in make-believe. Our worlds are only connected to bring us pain, shame, and remorse, while we ourselves are bringing satisfaction, enjoyment, and praise to others. You and I seem to be situated right where we are expected to be, worlds apart, and doing just what we are designated to do, keeping the system working, and the myth alive. It is this system of bipolar disorder that feeds upon the paradoxes on which our lives are forced to run, truth versus lies, hate versus love, parents versus vagrants, and so on. This is why I am glad and anxious to communicate to you through this letter now, my son, when you are old enough now to pause and think, and take the baton from me as I get ready for the fall, so that you can get yourself ready to hand over to your son. You see, this race in life that we are being forced to run is one, you will agree, of which we should have been in charge from the beginning, with one baton, one team, one philosophy, and one tape at the end to embrace. This race we are running, however, is organized to run differently. We are declared as members of the same team but only for convenience so that the confusion that follows is for the benefit and entertainment of others. We both are running in the opposite direction under the impression it is a relay, but we both have no baton and know not where the final tape ends to conclude our race or mission. We are both destined to be the laughingstock of our audience, especially when we clash in the middle of the field. We can be guaranteed to put up a great show, especially when we start to blame each other for going in the wrong direction and for having no baton for the race. Your recognition of me is based on what you have been told, even though we had met on those prescribed or mandated occasions when it was safe for you and me to put on our act that we were father and son. Our better moments were always tainted with a flash of anger from you for no apparent reason, after which I regretted I had ever troubled you with my presence or my presents, and that your behavior was growing stranger by the day. I knew that subsequently we would entertain everyone with our misgivings or desperation. Eventually, I stayed away to give you a rest and time away from me so that you can be returned to your usual conditioning comfortably. If you hesitate to read my letter or dump it into the trash because you suspect my intention is to poison your mind against your mother in retaliation for what I think she has done with you, then you are mistaken. It is too late and unwise to do so at this stage. What I have to say in this letter has to do absolutely with you and you only. Whatever I have to mention about your mother, sisters, or brothers are only relative for reference to what I have to say concerning you. My mission is too important or urgent to get it entangled with substances for a vendetta against your mother I had once loved and the offspring of what was once a relationship of hope and promise. If you think on the other hand that there is some secret benefit I am about to derive from this exercise, let me put your mind at ease about what it is, or could be. First of all, if you merely just accept and read it, I will have succeeded in fulfilling one of my life's missions to pass that baton from father to son. That baton is symbolic of my inner thinking, my aspirations, my philosophy, and my wisdom of a life well or badly spent. Fathers cannot help it, son; it is in the genes of all living male species, especially mammals. There are mothers or females and there are fathers or males who have roles to fulfill to their offspring. If you had not survived to this age, I would have been forced to adopt a substitute son or sons because of the very natural inclination beyond my control. You would be forced to do the same if I had not passed it on to you. A substitute will be just a patchwork of selected pieces of a big puzzle that will remain a puzzle. Regardless of what I give to the hundreds of youths that I teach, they have to select the pieces to fill in the mysteries of the emptiness in their lives. I am saving you that ordeal of having to do what millions of men and boys your age are compelled to go through because of this epidemic of separation or division of families that plagues our society today. Your genes are my genes, and it is your human right to know how and why you are the way you are and be proud to accept it and live with it. Any system or person that attempts to prevent you from making contact with your father, or, even under circumstances, understanding who he is, is guilty of committing a crime against humanity and is bent on some form of exploitation. In order to win your sympathy for their cause and get you to hate me at the same time, they tell you that I have committed the crime of neglecting you. How come every process and every system were so rigidly bent on suppressing any good information about me, hunting me down like a common fugitive, even after I have given of my best, and making me fear for my life, my career, my good name just for being responsible for bringing you into this world? They say that it is inevitable that they do it for your sake, for your well-being and protection. An entire support system of social workers, psychologists and therapists, educators and lawmakers, politicians and scholars, got involved in the witch hunt, for the children's sake, they say. Have they considered where they have you sitting at the front seat of this torture chamber, what is happening to you internally as a person, as a male, who will one day become a father? I have seen and heard other fortunate fathers sit on these death panels vehemently ridiculing other fathers and advocating harsher penalties equivalent to the inquisition of the dark ages. They are applauded as heroes and role models too, and no one seems to have the courage to even ask the basic questions: "Are these men not human beings too? Will these enforcements build family unity now and in the future? Can love and responsibility be enforced by law and coercion? How can these decisions affect our young men of today and their response to family life later?" The questions can go on and on, son, but nobody is asking them. If they did, they were never loud enough to save the millions of fathers being declared imbeciles and "deadbeats" and all the other derogative inhuman labels simply because they developed problems with their relationships and their financial obligations.

Now that I may have succeeded in getting your attention, you may want to ask why I selected you instead of your older brother. Well, that part is easy for me to answer but hard for me to explain. I just have that gut feeling that your older brother is not ready for this level of commitment and the younger ones are still growing. You are just about ready, but not quite, but I have grown weary of holding the mantle and waiting for someone to qualify; your brothers will arrive there one day, even after it will be too late. I trust you will be some comfort to them. They are too busy now chasing after role models and substitutes and dreams of what is acceptable manly behavior dictated by their mother and the system. I can imagine them going to church with their eyes peeling at posters and male church leaders, pumping up muscles for ball games and looking up to their coaches, and searching into movies for "he-man" stars for super roles they can adopt. You were different in some ways. You had two broken relationships and stand at the crossroads of your own life. You saw how easy it was for a woman's displeasure to plunge you straight into prison, and now you have a son and his mother has taken off her mask. I heard you say that you swore to your sister that your life will be better and different in the New Year. Well, son, I wish you had sworn to yourself and not to your sister, because a woman's expectations are obviously different from those of a man's. Moreover it does not happen that easy as you think because you were resolute and committed. If your mentor gives you the impression that it is that easy, tell him your father said he is not telling you the whole truth. Perhaps when he hears what I said he may be more frank and honest and begin to advise you better.

CHILDHOOD

When I was with the family, I said to you boys that your life will be tougher than mine, and you all burdened me with questions to explain. I did not really intend to scare you that way, only to make a point to get your attention. What I really meant to say was that we in our time had fewer issues to deal with in almost every area in our lives. We had the same kinds of problems but fewer issues that went with them. To begin with my father, he was by far less educated than I am today yet conducted himself with such a high level of sophistication you would assume he had a college education. I hardly saw him reading a book, yet every day after work he would examine his music sheets and make arrangements for his band. As a musician, he played the saxophone but could also play every other instrument in his band. I had no need to admire Glen Miller, Count Basie, Duke Ellington, or Dave Brubeck because I had them all at my fingertips when my father's band played. I heard the music arranged in our sitting room and he often asked me to help him keep time with the drum. He tried his best to get me to blow into the saxophone, but I wanted to draw, although I liked the music. I was perhaps too used to him taking care of me to realize I needed a mother too. I felt he did a marvelous job because I knew nothing else. For many years my brother, sister, and I enjoyed a calm, protected, and fulfilled life with a single parent. For one thing the protection was there. My father, your very grandfather, was like a terrible warrior, a raging vigilante and advocate for the weak and oppressed. He was quick to champion other people's problems and plunge himself into the foreground to fight for their cause, even if it included physical confrontation. People feared and respected his tenacity and vehemence when he was preoccupied with a mission. I feared it too that one day he could have been assassinated by the enemies whose plans he had spoiled. Your grandfather's philosophy was that you had to make war to get peace. There was peace all right. Our entire neighborhood was quiet and peaceful because of his warlike influence.

The other side of him that we knew was even better. He was home every night helping us settle down in the evenings, sharing in the preparation of dinner, and joking like a comedian. He would have us laughing all the way to bed, telling us stories, and I mean stories that linger in our minds that seemed to last forever. He was so convincing and charismatic that we hated when the nine o'clock theme song came on the radio and he would usher us all into bed. We loved and admired our dad and could not get enough of him. His strict disciplinarian style was so very simple to adhere to, we hardly ever got into conflict with him. Once in a while, like children, we would forget conveniently and had to be reminded. We all had our assigned chores and helped each other to avoid any chance of getting him upset. For a man who bred terror on the outside as a community advocate, he was more like a gentle giant when dealing with our shortcomings. Corporal punishment was almost never used, although the very thought of it would scare us to death anyway. Instead he employed the strategy of intrinsic discipline that would be considered too sophisticated for his quality of education, and they were very simple for us to understand and live up to. When, for example, we asked permission to go to the community center grounds to play, he would promptly consent but simply say, "Remember." One day he made us observe the birds and the animals heading home at sunset. We did not get the point until he belabored the fact that the animals knew it was time to go home and that no one had to remind them. He even made us observe it for ourselves. He did not have to remind us again, since it was too obvious to ignore. He never had any reason to help us with our school homework because he had trained us to be very independent. It was not a case of if we had done our homework, but why we had not. He would remind us never to leave our teachers at school to come home if there was something taught we did not understand. He probably would not have known how to help us anyway if he had to, but since the responsibility of accountability was ours, he did not have to.

This level of expectation pervaded into almost every aspect of our relationship with him, our growing up as children and our interaction with our neighbors. He would for a while pretend not to see, and then he would confront us with a question. In finding an answer for him, we had the responsibility to solve the problem. He disliked, for example, how our neighbors across the street lived with unkempt house and lawns and litter everywhere, while they sat around all day in idle gossip. He never forbade us from socializing with them, except that he insisted we should not exchange visits, lend or borrow anything from them, and share any of their idle gossips. Whenever we had surplus vegetables from our kitchen garden, he would encourage us to include them in our giveaways so that every neighbor was treated the same. He made us recognize the importance of being tolerant without being submissive, repugnant, or haughty. Our neighbors probably never knew what we really thought about them, but because of observing their lifestyle, we kept ourselves busy doing our chores or doing something constructive even when we had our leisure. Except when we went to school or the community center, we played with each other in our home or in the yard. We had a flower garden which we seemed to have transformed in our minds into an enchanted forest and invented all kinds of games and imaginary scenarios to suit our childish fancies. My sister and I were great singers and would practice our duets for the school Christmas concert or the next church service.

Even our chores were flavored with fun and fond memories. When my brother threw feed for the chickens, we would see birds of all description come out of nowhere to join them and we would get excited about the new birds we discovered for that year. My fish pond was also a center of attraction at fish-feeding time, when we would see the tilapias emerge from their hiding places to grab the feed. My brother and sister would help me to harvest the green vegetables from our kitchen garden, and we would sort them and prepare the extras to give out to neighbors nearby. Helping my older sister prepare dinner for the evening was the greatest fun of all. We dictated our own menus based on the ingredients we had at home. Since we had our own homegrown chickens, eggs, green vegetables, root vegetables, and fish, it was easy to design any combination of these to suit our fancy and taste. We helped each other so that we would all be ready to have dinner together. By the time dinner was ready, my father would have arrived or he would have been there earlier on the porch practicing on his saxophone. He would eat whatever we had prepared, although sometimes he would join us in the kitchen and teach us a few cooking techniques. Our grandmothers and aunts taught us how to wash and iron our clothes, and we grasped that so easily that very soon we prepared our own school uniforms. My father merely inspected them after we had them on already to leave for school. He would scrutinize our overall appearance with the calm fortitude of an army general, and yet it was a pleasant experience to have him check for the finest detail such as a slack button, a loose hem, or a dull shoe.

With all the freedom and independence we enjoyed with our father, we knew he had his own way to employ his checks and balances. He delegated me, the older son, to be in charge of the house in his absence. That was a huge responsibility for the son of a fearless warrior and community vigilante, to maintain that alertness and sense of reverence for the home when he was away at work. I had to convince myself that I was doing a great job, even just for my sister's sake. Young men were milling around like hounds, whistling and trying to get her attention. The temptation was probably great for her, but the ferocious tenacity with which I stayed alert kept them at bay. These young men were older schoolmates and were taller and bigger than I was, but I would much prefer to go through hell facing or even fighting them than be confronted with my father's anger and disappointment. Before long, what started as pretense to scare bigger opponents developed into a true temperament of a boy warrior always championing the cause of the weak against the strong. I had numerous fights with the older boys defending younger schoolmates and very rapidly developed a reputation as a boy vigilante that made me very popular at school, like my father was in the community. My father never punished me for fighting, although he would ask me every detail of the story. Sometimes I would detect a slight grin on his face that indicated that he agreed with my judgment or that he was proud of my actions as a son of his. I was so proud and grateful for him as a father, showing off my courage and moral tenacity was one way to give back to him for the fortitude we enjoyed in our lives. Occasionally my classmates and I would be enjoying our recess and he would show up with a little snack which I would share with my friends. I knew, however, that it was one of his regular checkups on us, to inspect our clothing and check on our behavior at school. Except for my regular vigilante fighting, the teachers were high in their praises for us, making my father even more proud of us.

During the course of my early childhood and even until my preteen years, since our lifestyle was so firmly built around our father, I did not feel the need for the presence of a mother. As children, we could not explain it then, but that need was beginning to grow upon us, and for the first time we began asking questions about her, whether she was alive or why she never visited us. I suspect that my sister who had become a teenager probably needed her more, and my younger brother craved for the bonding, but I was too preoccupied being tough like my father and taking care of business when he was gone. My grandmothers and aunts mentored my sister a lot, teaching her the finer skills of housewifery and fine grooming, but I overheard them referring to my mother and the need for my father to get some woman to help him with us growing children. We were very opposed to the intervention of some stranger and almost took it for granted my father would not do it. We did not mind the temporary comforts with women who took turns to nanny us those nights when my father's big band had a concert, since we were never around them long enough to remember who they were. It never occurred to us whether he had an intimate lady friend or played the game of a playboy. We saw him last thing at nights and first thing in the morning and had no reason to suspect he went anywhere with anyone until one day we arrived from school and saw this woman and her daughter in our house and my father told us that she was there to live. We lived as two separate families for a few weeks until my father eventually asked them to leave. Then things changed dramatically when another woman arrived with her daughter. This time my father embraced her, but try as we did to accommodate her for our father's sake, it did not work. She was always complaining about something or another that we had done wrong and he would get frustrated and angry with us. She was persistent in her efforts and schemes to break that bond between us and our father. For some reason, she targeted my sister, and whatever she told my father he would react in uncontrollable rage toward my sister. For the first time I found myself torn between my loyalty toward my father and my sister. From our perspective, my father was gradually losing his sense of reason, so desperate he seemed to include this woman in his life. Even my aunts and grandmother tried convincing him that this match with this stepmother was not a good proposition, but my father remained defiant and proceeded to expel them from any further visits to our home.

Since the arrival of a stepmother, our home operated as two separate vacuums that only fused temporarily to accommodate my father. Even he spent most of his time at home now with his other family way into the evenings, only checking up on us to see whether we had done what we were supposed to do. Gradually my father's popularity dropped as the neighbors whispered and paid keen attention. Conflicts between my sister and the stepmother reached a climax, and we complained to our grandmothers and aunts. Even my uncles tried talking with my father. It was then that I started hearing rumors that my mother was alive, and my grandmother and aunts kept hinting that my sister would be better off with her mother. One day at school during recess, I was playing with my friends, as usual, when they suddenly stopped and stared at this strange woman standing and looking straight at us. When she introduced herself as my mother, I felt very embarrassed and did not know how to respond. We were trained to be wary of strangers, and now all my friends would realize that we never had a mother in our home. Behind the church next to our school was a graveyard, and it was rumored that spirits of the departed often revealed themselves during the day. After all, this woman was supposed to be dead, and here she was asking me to come to her. I refused, of course, until my principal invited me into his office and served as a mediator to connect us. When I told my father later about the incident, he was furious and fretted vehemently with himself for the rest of the evening.

I was able to observe how gradually my father's personality changed. He was no longer the calm, gentle giant that we admired and loved to be near. Instead, he avoided us and we avoided him, for fear of what he could be thinking or intending to do based on what this stepmother had told him. He had stopped practicing his music, and this was my favorite time with him while I did my drawings. The storytelling sessions before bedtime had stopped completely. After we finished our homework, we filled in that void by slipping into bed and talking ourselves to sleep. My sister was the one who lived with the greatest fear since she was the target of most allegations. My grandmothers advised that the next time my sister felt she was in danger; she should run away from home and come to their place. That happened soon enough one evening when my father arrived from work and went off into a fit of rage over what he had been told again, and as he stormed out of the house through the back door in search of something to beat her with, she slipped through the front door and disappeared like lightning into the night. He tumbled through the whole house looking for her. My sister never returned. The next thing I learned was that she was with our mother who had recently emerged from the "dead." My father's reputation in the neighborhood dropped even further since my sister left, as neighbors gossiped and avoided him on the street. The stepmother changed her tactics and tried showing affection to us two boys, and I pretended to accept her overtures because

I knew I had no choice. Even as a child I observed my father tumbling blindly all over himself and spending beyond his means in order to please her. He even purchased a car which he hardly needed. One day he got into an accident, wrecked the car, and sold it off for next to nothing. The next thing he did was to sell the house in which we lived, uprooted us from our calm and secured lifestyle, and moved us into the big city into a sublet apartment that in our minds felt more like a holding cell or cubicle for homeless or downtrodden people. My brother and I could not come to terms with living with several families in the same building sharing the same bathroom, kitchen, and sitting room. My father tried to explain to us that he had come to the city to pursue a better standard of living and opportunities for us, but we knew he had demoted himself into a daily worker earning less than a decent wage to cover his very basic expenses. The only person looking content was the stepmother who never worked. She earned some money by sewing for clients but was always busy going out when my father was not around. By then she and my father had started having regular quarrels about the shortage of money to do what she wanted. There was also a baby stepbrother joining the stepsister who was there. I had always done well in school and was about to do a major examination to qualify for high school. When I passed with honors, things took a turn for the worse with the stepmother as if I had committed a crime. She had told a friend she could not tolerate a legitimate child in the family doing better than her own, and she was going to do something soon to guarantee I do not excel again. That friend pleaded with us in secret to leave for fear of what could happen to us. By then, we had found out where my mother worked and lived and had even seen our sister one evening. I urged my brother to get his things, and we walked to where my mother worked. For her, our arrival was a pleasant surprise, although it complicated her life suddenly having to cater for a full-blown family with her small income. We adjusted well together in a lower flat of the huge Victorian bungalow her boss had allowed her to use at her job as a maid. With our country background and experience in self-reliance, especially in cooking, we were able to multiply her paltry dollars to make our living together more easy and comfortable. My only source of discomfort, however, was the horrible things that were being said about my father, perpetuated by my mother. Her aunt, her boss, her friends, and her church acquaintances all had this common notion of my father being such an ogre or demon. The stress went on and on hearing my father being described out of character for the person we knew, except when he came under the influence of the stepmother he had brought into our lives. I would not blame my sister to want to agree with what she heard, since she was the primary victim of the demise of the family at the time. I was very grateful for whatever sympathy people had for our situation or for whatever charitable contributions they had made to help us get settled, but that added ingredient of ridicule and disregard for my father was a real torture for me. I started to dislike my mother for circulating stories about her private life to evoke sympathy toward herself. I often observed her take on this pitiful, saintly posture of extreme hopelessness whenever people referred to her situation. Whenever that happened, I felt so humiliated and ashamed of being associated with her, that I was sore within me for days.

What surprised and disappointed me most about my mother was her inability to bond with us. Assuming, I suppose, her prayers were answered that we were all brought back to her, she took no advantage of her good fortune. Whenever she came from work, she avoided us, praying and reading her Bible and talking about demons that were sent by her enemies to torture her. Before my father got distracted and fallen from grace, in the evenings after dinner we would gather in the sitting room and share mock concerts with us. We would perform for him, and he would be the comedian and storyteller. It was the best time of our lives. Here we were anticipating a second spring of socializing with our mother, and here she was oppressing our spirits with this culture of gloom and doom, still praying for protection and retribution against unseen enemies. Occasionally we would try initiating some social interchange by talking about popular songs with her or even singing one to entertain her. After a short while she would grow reluctant or impatient and resort to her Bible reading and praying, shutting us out. We had to learn to adjust to the meager connection with her under the disguise that we were indeed getting a mother's love at last. We understood how her job would be important to her very existence, but my mother proved to be too pathetically submissive and dedicated to her job and her boss. She left absolutely no opportunity to even address a life of her own, except for reading her Bible and praying, of course. I pitied her condition and started to rebel against what I viewed in my mind as gross exploitation of my mother, even to the extent of slavery. She went upstairs before sunrise and never came back down to us until long after sundown. Even so, her salary was not even sufficient to pay a rent if she wanted to move to live on her own. When she complained to her boss about my protests, they both concluded that my father must have infected my mind with some of his devilish ideas. From then on I could not wait to graduate from high school and get away from that oppressive environment.

There, my son, is a sketch of any childhood as unpredictable, traumatic, enjoyable, and enlightening as yours. An old proverb says that a child is father of the man, and I think it is true that the experiences of our childhood shape our decisions, our personality, and our destiny as an adult. It does not happen merely because you had the experience, but because of what you consciously do with the experience, how you interpret it and how you respond to it. I did not dictate the circumstances, the actual experiences, or the results, but I can certainly decide how to shape myself and my personality based on what I learned from them, not on what they did to me. Life is a series of learning experiences for your guidance, growth, and inspiration. To miss those lessons offered you in life is to lay yourself out as a victim to be kicked around and trampled upon. How would you have dealt with my childhood experiences if you were in my place? Would you blame your grandfather for injecting that woman into his family, or would you blame your grandmother for leaving her children behind, creating the void? It may be very easy for you and me to speculate on the situation and arrive at a feasible answer. Your grandfather probably felt the need to fill the void in his life and heart and could have made a poor choice of a partner or lacked the leadership skills to make it work. It is not only what you do, but also how you do it. You may also have learned by now that even when all things appear to be perfectly fitted, a little discrepancy emerges, a little screw gets loose, and the discord that results can be phenomenal. Even as a child I could not imagine how my father programmed his mind to select, among all the women he knew, this particular woman to be the second partner in his life. Likewise, I could not imagine under what circumstances he had met my mother and how they saw it feasible to marry, much less to get the three of us from that union. I know for a fact that my mother was extremely beautiful and my father was like a rock star in the music world with huge demands for his presence. It was disappointing to see my hero and warrior of a father that I most admired fall from grace into disrespect, poverty, and shame. I still have the nostalgia of what he used to be, even as I see him today, a shell of his former self. My mother, I learned, had nourished dreams of being a movie star and probably could have become one if the timing and situation was right, but she had a very unhappy childhood with a cruel stepmother and a doting father. Regardless of what mistakes your grandparents made in their lives, remember that we as human beings are supposed to have the remarkable ability to adapt and recuperate from the downturns in our lives. That is what separates us from other species. Sometimes when the damage comes too early, it leaves obvious permanent scars, similar to my mother's, whose mother died when she was very young and her father replaced her with a tyrant. Sometimes the damage is more mental or psychological and is not that obvious. In the case of my father, whose parents were extensively rich and had no parenting skills or the moral training to make up for it, was left to carry out his childish whims and fancies in a brutish manner without any form of constraints or consequences. In your grandparents' time, the culture and the notion still prevailed, like in the dark ages, that is, when you were rich you were infallible, and your children could not be corrected or rebuked. Children of the rich were accountable to no one, and their parents enforced that. That was, I mean, illiterate rich parents, like my great-grandparents. They lost their wealth, of course, when my great-grandfather got sick, leaving behind a wild bunch of unruly children still grasping at illusions of having their own way with people and society and enforcing their own wishes by any means possible. My father's egomania found a positive outlet in him being a community leader and vigilante, but I could imagine that anyone who dared to challenge his ideas or opinions would arouse a raging tiger in him. My mother probably suffered a similar damage to her psyche when she was very young, and was perhaps a victim of physical and mental domination. Her immediate response was to submit and appeal for sympathy, and she had been stuck doing that ever since, even if she had to make up stories about my father tormenting her with demons all her life. For some of us humans in this life the damage done to us in our formative years had been so pervasive, the lessons we learned were acquired through panic and oppression, and we ran off into life limping from its aftereffects. Some of us have not had the opportunity to stop and take stock of our lives or the lessons we have learned because we had been too busy limping or hobbling along in the usual panic until we had come to accept it as normal and built our lesson about life based on it. Wisdom extracted through panic or in response to aggression is limited in value to those particular aspects of life only and should not be included in the general fundamentals for healthy living, I suppose. I think you would be very disappointed, my son, if all the wisdom I want to impart to you were based on reactions to what my grandparents, stepmother, mother, and her stepmother had done. I value my life and respect your intellect more highly than that, although I will still acknowledge that information about my background plays an important part in solving the puzzle of my own life. Son, you must remember always that what you do with information is more important than having it.

What do you suppose I could do with the knowledge I have about my father, mother, and grandparents? In what way do you think I should respond to my childhood experiences, especially when it took a downward turn from decisions my father had made? I could be judgmental and hate my parents and grandparents for setbacks in my life. What benefits would that have for me, except for me to grapple with my big ego and self-conceit at the expense of people to whom I owe the utmost respect? I could also use the knowledge as a learning experiment by speculating on how my life could have been different if my parents and grandparents were ideal and had made the right decisions. How do you suppose I could have prepared myself to inherit the riches my grandparents would have left for me? If my father had become established in the music world and my mother had become the movie star that she had dreamed of, what would I have done with my life at this time to complement that good fortune? With nothing to complain about, what would I adopt as my aspirations to live up to for the upliftment of humanity? No, son, I have not gone too far or aimed too high. Yes, when your goals are aimed high beyond yourself toward the good of all humanity, your objectives in life are sharpened with a higher sense of purpose. Those kinds of goals never fail regardless of circumstances. War and economic depression would strengthen them. Peace and tranquility would enrich them. The man who is involved in a passionate pursuit such as this through his plans, his actions, and his career can afford to live in the present and not gripe about the past or fear about the future. He will certainly be able to extend himself fully toward his family as the extension of his own self, as his contribution to humanity and the world.

I can almost hear you muttering under your breath to challenge me with a final question about my childhood before I move on to another phase of discussion. What is the major lesson that I have learned from my childhood? That is so ridiculously easy; I can never understand how it misses every aspect of government and society these days. The answer is the importance of a well-knitted, united family involving both a mother and a father. There are as many reasons why a child needs a father as a child needs a mother, and vice versa. If I knew why we were wired that way from evolution, except for the purpose of reproduction for the continuation of the species, I would forward it as my first argument. There is a natural instinct or drive or human tendency that compels us to care, protect, and love our offspring and prepare them for the next generation. The lower species demonstrate the need for this privilege, especially when they are held in captivity at the zoos or aquarium. There are findings from scientific and other research to establish how males and females are dedicated to support their offspring. Yet the highest species of planet Earth blessed with the greatest intelligence seem to miss this most important point. The family is the only single most potent power structure in any country or society, and the stability of any society can be diffused or become self-destructive when an integral part is missing or taken from that structure. In my case, it was the mother that was missing; in your case, it was the father. During my happier days with my father, the only thing I needed in my life then was my mother, although I did not realize it at that time. We needed the tender love and affection and the playful feminine sentiment of a good mother to balance the harsh, solid, aggressive, warlike sentiment of a good, heroic father. How else and where else can I best learn to be human and humane but during simple, silly, playful, and loving exchanges with my mother and father. Father, that symbol of authority, strength, force, and stability, is there at my disposal to protect, support, guide, and set limitations and standards for the family, and for me. How else, where else, and with whom will I feel the milk of human kindness ignite into electricity with only a gentle touch or a stare or a kiss on the cheeks, the warmth and fullness of the breast that fed me and the bosom that cradled me to sleep. My first true purpose for living and loving starts with responding to the aura of those two people who gave me my genes, my confidence, and my unique personality. My father and mother with a question and a smile can more expound life's principle to me than an army of social workers armed with bursting files and a senate of lofty speakers. How and why would I want to separate one from the other, embrace one and despise the other, connect with one and substitute the other, when the blood of both flow through my veins? Childhood can be so much like the beginning of heaven on earth if Mother and Father get the right support and compliments for being themselves. Allowing that structure to dissolve could be like connecting what is left to the doors of hell.

Son, can you imagine a human being growing up as a child without that wholesome connection of family life, pass an entire decade of his or her life, plagued with an atmosphere of insecurity, hypocrisy, and violence? Can you imagine being coerced, encouraged directly or indirectly, into condemning one of your parents, only to regret later in life because you realized that you have been actually condemning yourself? Can you imagine the void you feel within you when you conclude that your life is nothing more than a routine of being shuffled from day cares, to nannies and to schools? What would you suggest a child who had been deprived of the experiences of a wholesome normal childhood do when he or she stands at the threshold of adolescence? How would you expect that child to face the future with confidence and a strong sense of purpose? How would a child even know what to give back what he or she had never been given in the first place?

ADOLESCENCE

This is the best and worst of times for you. It is the best because the possibilities are endless for happiness and achievements, and you have all of your youth and energy before you. It is the worst because you have just come out of childhood and have not learned enough to help you harness that energy, enthusiasm, and imagination for your benefit and best interest. You might not have noticed it then, but you would have developed a strong sense of overconfidence to the extent where you begin to offend or win the admiration of those around you. This is where both your education and your home upbringing would help you to develop some power of constraints. Remember, son, that no kind of quality education or upbringing can guarantee that you would make the right decisions or act in the right way at this stage of your life, or for the rest of your life. A good education is what you give to yourself and not necessarily what the teachers or your parents belabor themselves to give to you. With all that money, infrastructure, teaching, and testing, educational endeavors are all based on assumptions, if not illusions, that you want to learn and that they are preparing you for a future condition they know will exist. The overemphasis on rudimentary academic skills and knowledge is one way in which one generation of planners catered for the next. It is equivalent to saying that your parents are preparing you for a precise future they know will exist when you reach their age so that all you have to do is conform and perform as you were programmed to do. I agree with you, son, that some parents even start preparing their children from childhood for college. This is the time you will notice people begin to reveal certain expectations of you they had never mentioned before. If you are part of the revolving circle that fits the expectations, they will embrace you, praise you, uplift you, and say all manners of nice things about you. On the other hand, if you are too independent and radical in the direction you are going, they will descend to ridiculous measures to show their dissatisfaction. Change can be a very scary proposition to parents, teachers, and even political leaders. It is easier to keep things fixed and revolving as they are because it can easily be controlled and monitored to assign people to function to keep it that way. Some people apologetically and mistakenly call it culture and tradition. There is even a system of punishment and rewards included with it. For those who conform, there will be jobs and scholarships to earn and graduations to attend with lots of regalia and vanity.

In a way, it is advantageous to conform, since a job will be waiting, and doors will open mysteriously and timely, ushering you to where you are supposed to or expected to be. Obviously, things are geared to stay the way they always were, and there are no incentives for flexibility. That is why for those who do not conform, the penalty is so brutal. Son, they do not put it that bluntly to you at first, but people who do not conform are indirectly doomed to a life of poverty, crime, and finally, jail. I was doing extremely well at school, and when I graduated it was taken for granted by everybody I knew that I would continue excelling in the academic field and become a professor at college, a lawyer, or a doctor. I hated the idea of spending the rest of my life doing any one of these, and when I said finally what I wanted to be, most people were disappointed and shocked. I wanted to be an artist. That was not even regarded as a profession in those days. I probably would have felt better settling to be a musician into which my father had tried to lure me. To make this important decision, you will need to focus on what is important for you and your future and pursue the kind of education best capable of giving you the necessary knowledge and skills to enhance your abilities in that field. You will notice the priority I am giving to education. I suspect that while you had been growing up, you might have been very playful and missed a few essential clues and skills. Now you will have to make up for it. Check your academic skills that they are sharp and on track. If they are not, you owe that responsibility to yourself to make up for it immediately.

Son, I run the risk of you getting upset with me, but adolescence is such a crucial onset into life there is no room for mistakes. I can tolerate you making mistakes going in the right direction, since they can still be building blocks for progress. The mistakes I cannot tolerate are those geared in the wrong direction. This is your stage in life for having grand illusions. They are great motivators, and the mask they wear can captivate you and bring you to the brink of reality too late in your life. By now you ought to honor the difference between a dream and a reality. You can dream about winning awards or being a movie star, but you have to work directly toward becoming a pilot, an engineer, or any other career where you can be in complete control of how you get there. The only way you can exercise that control is if you exercise the discipline and tenacity of spirit to fulfill the requirements to get there. In all you do, however, make certain that that goal is worth your effort. That, again, is easy by standards we discussed before. Is this goal all about you alone, looking good, impressing the world with yourself, doing something spectacular that would be of benefit to you? Or will it be a goal in which you have discovered a great need in your community, the country, or the world in which you can make a great change for the better to benefit a large number of people? It is not enough to know where the need is, but also how you begin to prepare yourself with the skills to make a difference. Finally, it is what you do in your first few steps. To make your life worthwhile, it is you who have to make living your life worth the while. I hope, however, I have said enough to help you avoid making the first mistake and spend the rest of your life trying to correct it through the other mistakes that follow.

You may have noticed I have not mentioned the word "college" yet, not because I do not think it is important or anything like that. You need to prepare yourself to be in an environment of higher learning by starting college, but merely being in college does not make you college material, unless you came with your own mission and purpose and the necessary tools to fulfill them, even before you first stepped through its doors. College definitely does not transform anybody, and this fashionable notion that college is the utopia to a world of success and happiness in life is a blatant myth. If there is one thing you should discover, shortly after you settle down in college, you will discover that for yourself. On some occasions, some students who are late bloomers get their first true awakening of themselves while on campus doing a course or having an extraordinary experience or encounter with someone. If you tell me that you are taking basic courses to acquire basic skills and information related to your interests, then you have my undivided attention. Please do not assume that a college education can be taken lightly or that you can acquire specialized training on your own only by being smart and committed. Everything has its time and place and proper order. If you want to be a doctor, you will first need to qualify for entry into medical school, spend your time training like anyone else, and get properly certified. That goes for any other profession or area of specialization you want to pursue. You cannot improve or reinvent anything to which you had never been properly exposed.

Therefore, son, if you are not going to college just to be in fashion, to look good, or to keep up appearances, you are on the right track. Remember that at this stage of your life, you have to make all the judgments and decisions for everything around you. Things are not always what they seem; regardless of how real and convincing they appear in your very eyes. People do not always mean what they say, in spite of how genuine they speak or pleasant they behave. Your parents protected you from this kind of political abuse when you were young. Now is the time for you to assert your independence and take charge of your first lessons in life. Never believe, for example, all you see, hear, and read in an advertisement, even about college and its programs. Research it, and then check it out for yourself, even if it involves interviewing the professors. Even so, since you have the least information and experience at this stage about the subject, they can dominate and mislead you with predigested information. If you do not get it right, some academic advisor may quickly convince you to enroll into courses and activities to suit the priorities for his or her job or the benefit of the department he or she represents. Could you imagine the possibility of being coerced to commit your time, money, energy, loyalty, and enthusiasm to a course or activity that hardly concerns your personal goals and aspirations? That is like beginning the race of your life and career running in the wrong direction. Your mentors and advisers may be your eyes and ears, but the final decision, along with the consequences and rewards that follow, rests with you.

I know this is the time when you need your parents most, to help guide you through this crucial period, but even the best of parents with the best of intentions find it difficult to leave their world behind to look ahead for you. We the parents often rely too much on concepts and notions of the past over which we had or assumed control of the basis on which to assess and plan for the future. As logical and practical as that may seem, it does not cater for the factors of change and circumstances that are continuously changing the dynamics of what seems to be the same before our very eyes. In some cases your parents, relatives, and close friends would be more of a hindrance in helping you to negotiate these first steps into the future. For you to negotiate the future it is necessary to reexamine and renegotiate the past in your mind so that you can visualize a future that is yours, based on your perception, your aspiration, and your needs. You will need to create a future of your own, based on a world you perceive evolving. Even as parents we will have to trust your judgment, your foresight, and your intuition; but for most of us parents this is very difficult to do because our confidence is very much embedded in our experiences and accomplishments of our past. Our weakness at this stage is a mixture of egotism, fear, and selfishness. We fear we will be forgotten and neglected after all we have done for our community, our family, and the world and look forward to you to be our ambassador and advocate. That pledge of allegiance can be so demanding, it can feel like a declaration of war against you and your future aspirations. Son, forgive us and the world if it feels that way to you. Do not become distracted by our agitations. We need to get ourselves weaned from our inner selves so that we can look clearly ahead for you. When you choose to do a course or a major toward a career or spend endless hours in the library or laboratory researching a topic, I want to feel excited that something new and big for the future has started in a small way by you. I want to feel that somewhere and sometime soon, because of you and the choices you made, the world will become better some way that you dictated because of your mission and your passion in something that you are doing. You do not need a degree from college to do that, although it will satisfy certain sections of society if you do. You can spend half your life in college and do nothing of significance. On the other hand, you may not spend a day in college, yet because of what you are doing, scholars and professors in college campuses all over the world may exhaust themselves trying to keep pace with you.

If these aspirations sound a little too far-fetched for you, then I hope they will not remain that way for very long, or I fear I will certainly lose you, my son. There has been so much emphasis these days being placed on the importance of a college education that most people seem to believe that it is ideal and appropriate to invest their life's earnings and savings in their child's education. Even from as early as kindergarten the frantic preparation begins. Schools have been converted into industrial academic machines, fine-tuning and mechanizing the rituals of the learning processes and concepts to utmost precision and timing. Generations of mindless graduates are capped like soda bottles and conveyed to the next level of their conditioning up into the utopia of their glory even before true learning begins. After the grand speeches, the uproars send the caps like cannons to swarm the sky. It is only after then that some of them begin to question what they had been doing in college, or even to realize that they had been doing their learning in the wrong way. If it happens to you, my son, and you do not recover in time, you may never know what is happening to you. Learners who graduated en masses from caged and regimented systems eventually find ways to compensate for their lack of individuality. Too many of our valuable graduated minds can be lost that way trying to find themselves back to their world, even after they have landed a good job and settled down with a family.

If you suspect that you feel that way, son, it may be partly because of the education you were given, both at home and at school. Some of us may continue to prolong the hype of our educational upbringing through the jobs we acquire and not recognize the difference. Factories need to make quick outputs to generate profits and satisfy customers and investors. Worker satisfaction and well-being are the least of the priorities. Schools likewise have to show good test results to please parents and politicians and compete with other states and other schools. The overemphasis on safety, documentation and testing can easily be mistaken for concern for the children themselves. What were the children doing in the meantime? Where was the investment toward your youth, energy, and creativity, and other qualities you posses that you needed to learn skills to target a high sense of value for morality, production, and perfection? Schools could in fact have been regimenting entire generations of learners away from their personal goals and aspirations. With all those endless experimentation and documentation of teaching methodologies and styles, school systems still needed quick, rapid results reflected more through what data say than what children have become. If only they had invested more in developing strategies to help children to learn how to learn, then school operations and children will be so much different. Higher-sounding virtues like responsibility and accountability would have started from kindergarten as simple games pervading every subject and every human need. Subjects become, therefore, types of raw materials through which children challenge themselves, their teachers, and their community. Children could have been engaged in learning how to learn while being responsible themselves for their own learning, from as early as kindergarten. Son, can you imagine how much fun there would have been in learning in schools where children are mobilized to fulfill expectations they sanctioned for themselves, with or without the help of teachers? When a subject matter is dispensed among young learners for them to incorporate into various aspects of daily living, both learning and the material that is learned assume a meaning and function relevant to their lives. This is what I insist school should have had you and me doing so that making adaptations to what we learn and what we can do with it to better our lives become second nature to us all. This is what I call a functional education that matures naturally to functional living. Schools cannot prepare us for the future. They can only help us to develop the skills and potentials to do so.

Let us both be careful, though, not to make excuses for our own deficiencies and limitations and blame it on our schools and teachers, or even our parents. Our teachers have done their best, based on what they knew and under the circumstances. They are doing that even now. They may be honest and sincere and deeply committed, I am sure, and will keep doing what they are doing into the future and feel absolutely certain that they are right. Sorry to confuse you a little, but they are right, for now. However, they are not right for the future, for you and your children's generation. That is where the problem is and will always be. Even the purest water left standing still, will stagnate. Similarly, any system that does not flow, regardless of how good it is, will breed all sorts of evil setbacks, unless it is built to evolve inherently in the process of change. Mankind himself will never be perfect, but he is perpetually bound to strive toward that perfection. I know that it is little comfort that all of us will come to the end of our days and never see the peak of perfection of anything, any system or even ourselves. However, striving for perfection is man's highest goal. Learning how to make this world a better place than we met it should be our mission.

If you have managed to survive reading up to this far into my letter, I am very grateful that I have not lost you yet. However, it gets harder for me to go on bringing the harsh realities to you about the world in which we live. That is, you have to be prepared to go it alone. Son, it is by far easier to leave things as they are and to protect, support, and maintain the status quo. Consequently, the system will be able to operate without question or interference from generation after generation. Again, son, it may seem so, but it is not. The truth is that a few people will always benefit at the expense or inconvenience of the masses. The next generation is not obligated to suffer so that a few people can be comfortable, and you will have friends, in high places, middle places, and low places. If you can develop the constitution to turn a blind eye to the suffering of the mass of humanity, you will notice that you have to change your line of thinking to even begin to be or feel comfortable. By then, I will have lost you, since you will be surrounded by too many friends of a certain type. All that I had written before will be forgotten, and burned, so that you could feel comfortable with a lifestyle you have chosen. Even I will fear for my own safety not because of what I had done, but because of who I am and what I believe. Welcome to the real world of good and evil. If you cannot afford to turn a blind eye to the suffering of humanity around you, then you have your mission cut out for you. Welcome to the inevitable world of politics, the only channel through which you can achieve your goal. There will be many cheerleaders, well-wishers, donors, and disciples, but you must never forget that you are always alone.

In the real world of politics, you get the insights into human nature. The fairy-tale storybook characters you viewed as a child begin to transform before your very eyes, and you will be able to unpeel the layers of truth in circumstances and the true identities of leaders and followers, lawmakers and henchmen. You will revisit history with passion, and with a great sense of urgency, to find solutions to problems and calm your troubled spirit. The way you will begin to live your life will be one huge paradox. You will be glad to talk with your enemies for the real fun of it and will hide from your friends, even at dinnertime. By now it will become clear to you why I hinted that you will have to be prepared to be alone in life's real ventures. Human beings are basically very selfish and will go to immoral extremes to satisfy their greed and lust. Laws and ideologies have not been able to curb the human appetite for conflict and domination of his own kind. There is only one key solution to the problem of mankind and his uncanny behavior and tendencies: leadership. I mean strong, good leadership. Mankind's greatest need is leadership. Just as good and evil is part of our individual character, so will it express itself in society through the actions of mankind. An individual bound and committed to a high ideal for living will strive for high standards of living, guided and motivated by his or her own initiatives. When large numbers of people in a society get attracted and committed to higher ideals, their lives and the community in which they live reflect those ideals. A good leader will assemble an army of people who embody those ideals and send them off in a crusade to transform the world. No, son, I am in no way referring to the kinds of bloody crusade from the dark ages fostered by hate, greed, and religious fanaticism. Crusades can be good, bloodless, and blessed with enlightenment, peace, and love. One good leader can initiate and maintain such a movement. Such a movement is not stuck on petty details and issues but is driven by high ideals, principles, and standards. People will join such a movement not because they are driven merely by selfish motives for short-term satisfaction, but by ideals and aspirations that are self-fulfilling and gratifying.

If you aspire to be a good leader, then your first obligation is to be a good follower. You do this at school, work, and play in the activities in which you are involved now. Good followers are not blind ones, gullible for every fad or theory to excite a sluggish mind. You can be part of a movement, for example, in your career or profession, dedicated to cure a disease or this world's problems. That is the kind of loneliness that wins the greatest crowd, when you are part of the solution of a bigger problem that will change the world, and you are so convinced that you continue to do your best regardless of those you do not see working alongside you. Being part of a team does not lessen your commitment to your personal standards or open doors for compromises or surrender based on what others have not done. Classmates may sarcastically call you a nerd, and working colleagues may gang up to frustrate you, but remember that in the real battle in life men earn their rank according to the tenacity of their will, even to do it alone, if necessary. The greatest of all battles is fought in a place of solitude, deep in the head and heart, when you have to conquer your own fears and shortcomings to fulfill your convictions to yourself. Other people may be involved in the same mission with you, but their commitment is never the same as yours, regardless of how convincing they may speak or act. Unless you are convinced otherwise, it is safe for your sanity to take for granted that people get involved in movements and missions for some reason that is of particular benefit to them in one way or another and that their motivation, behavior, and loyalty are linked to the extent to which they feel their goals are being fulfilled. That is why it is important not to get yourself distracted by what people say or feel about you. Try to understand and empathize with them, for, after all, they are also part of the bigger solution of a human problem. To get angry or frustrated with them is to miss the point. They may indirectly to be crying out to you for help after becoming conscious of their limitations or weaknesses, but they may also want desperately for you to succeed to boost their own inner reserve to try. In being negative or judgmental toward other people, you weaken the movement, the mission, the unifying spirit, and yourself in your endeavors. Your pride and your ego can be the greatest hindrance to your growth as a man, as a professional, and as a leader. Look at the bigger picture, but keep a close watch on the little details. Applaud and encourage the strong, and give that wiling hand to help the weak, the needy, and even those that strayed in the wrong direction. Events in your life may operate like one huge wheel beyond your control, but every little incident within your grasp may be that missing bearing that helps to make the connections and meanings for the wheel to turn smoothly. These are your guiding angels that come to you in the most unusual way under the most unexpected circumstances. The clues to the world's most important problems are concealed in the most insignificant events. Architects and industrial designers look at mini models of their big ideas to further analyze, examine, and invite fresher ideas to improve and expand even further. The only difference with life's big ideas is that they have already been worked out by some supreme intelligence beyond our comprehension. All we need to do is just find the switches or the clues and turn them on. However, human beings are so preoccupied with fulfilling petty needs and settling grievances, they tumble over each other as if blindfolded, missing the clues right within their reach and the opportunity to log in to make the world into a heavenly place. Just as a tiny atom, smaller than the eye can see, comprises the big things our eyes do see, even so the seemingly insignificant, meaningless event, person, or thing has the potential to dictate the fate of a people, a civilization, or even the world.

EDUCATION

A good education does not begin and end in or around school but encompasses all the experiences we have in our lives at school, at home, and in our community. What your father and mother do with you, around you, and for you are some of the first and foremost lessons that will shape your personality and help determine the choices of what meanings you will give or extract from the other encounters you will have. Do you remember when we used to go jogging and we stopped to observe a toad crushed flat on the roadway? We had a conversation about that toad and you used that occasion to reinforce the pedestrian rule of crossing the road: "Look left, look right, and look left again, and then walk briskly across." Since then, you were always alert when we were on the road and always held my hand for us to cross the road. The encounter with the crushed toad was an education about road safety, but it translates symbolically to everything else we do in this life. You do not have to wait for a life to be battered to get the message about what you are supposed to do to succeed and protect yourself. Too many people in my time had resigned themselves to an education confined to an institution or a school with an assembly of teachers, professors, or persons with elaborate public or academic credentials. They failed, however, to understand the significance of simple things before their very eyes and got crushed in life because they had not seen the pitfalls and the carcasses. A mother who stops with her three-year-old in front of the supermarket door to get her child to learn the entrance and exit door before they enter is doing the same thing I did as a parent when we encountered the crushed toad. There are different lessons based on the same principles that we will continue to encounter for the rest of our lives. Education should be a way of life and living that should guide our every action and influence the choices we make. When you were very young, your father and mother performed different roles to help give you that peripheral vision of life and the human interaction that went with it. There is an underlying moral foundation to all these rituals we perform as a family that is crucial for our very existence, our survival, and our enrichment. This is the crucial element that outlines our social values. In education these days there is much talk about intelligence and expertise and proficiency in a frantic competition to achieve the highest test scores. All of these test scores are worth little or nothing without a sound moral foundation established within a wholesome family, nurtured by a mother and father. There is no sound intelligence without morality, and no education is worth the credential it boasts unless it brings us closer to our sense of purpose in this life and our obligation to humanity. When the time comes and you have a son or daughter and you commit yourself to sacrifice a huge part of your earnings to save for his or her college education or special tutoring, you must ask yourself if that child of yours appreciates why you are so exhausted at the end of the day. It is never too early to lay this foundation for education that is the engine that drives the kind of self-esteem and academic proficiency that can hardly be outclassed.

Does a good education necessarily result because you attended the best school or came into contact with a highly qualified instructor? An inquiry of this type, you will find, tends to draw you back into a whirlpool of questions about the truth that can engage you forever with an unsatisfactory answer. Whether you get sucked down to the lowest ebb of your patience or anxiety or you spiral off up into the heavens assuming you have discovered some new realm of knowledge or happiness, this inquiry focuses on topics or issues that are very personal and emotional and is the foundations on which our very life and future are grounded. The problem is that most of us feel more confident to assess our education only after we get it. By then it is already too late, because we are forced to use the very analytic tools that same education had given us. The concept of good, for example, is very relative to what we had been cultured to accept or believe is good, and this mental attitude will prevail in all the important aspects of our life and living. Being in a good school or college is like being in the company of scholars or wise men. That experience or position means nothing until the nature of your engagement with them and them with you result in some form of enlightenment of all parties involved. Once you believe in something or some institution to the extent that you are unwilling to question and analyze its functions and purpose, or its agents, such as teachers that exercise power over you, then you are on the way to getting a bad education and using it to give yourself tools for life and living that will produce much pain and anguish for the rest of your life.

Son While I doubt there can ever a perfect system of education, you can still make a perfect match between your goals and what a school provides if you can remain committed to yourself throughout the process. I can only speculate on what it should be and how to feel your way to open its golden doors to the companions and mentors you must follow along its path. You will undoubtedly have to prepare yourself to begin such a journey, for you will most likely be on this highway of knowledge for the rest of your life. These preparations have very little to do with your career, the school itself, or the teacher. It has to do with you, what you stand for and what you are committed to embrace in the future. If you are sincere in your quest to learn and improve in whatever capacity you will serve, your actions and deportment will be so magnetic, those connected with the journey you will take will not be able to resist the temptation of aligning themselves with you. You should not let yourself get distracted or intimidated with references to intelligence and expertise in this or that area of study. The main precursor to intelligence is morality that qualifies or judges man in all endeavors. A man who is predisposed to do nothing but what is wholesome and right for the upliftment of humanity has already, by so doing, induced himself with nuclear energy to fire his ambitions beyond the limitations of the conventional world. He will stand at the door of the treasures of knowledge and discover the true purpose and functions of schools, their professors, and the progress they provide. He will open the door to begin his process of refinement, not because of what some institution or person is about to give him, but what he is about to give himself.

Son, I should feel comfortable and assured that you would do well now that you are about to go to college, but I have some apprehensions that restrict my enthusiasm. I was one of those idealists who were obsessed with this grand illusion that college was this beacon of hope in which the cream of every society would embrace the higher aspirations of finding solutions to mankind's most grievous problems. I had every reason to be, since I was given a scholarship and high expectations were placed on me. I was privileged to be in this exalted place where the best brains can mentor an army of liberators and problem solvers bent on the same mission to attend to the needs of humanity and raising the standards of how we treat the environment and coexist among ourselves. I must admit that they had not turned a blind eye to the problems of the world. Instead, it seemed to me that what they were preoccupied doing is findings ways to exploit them, compiling data and reports, and using the miseries of the less fortunate to advance a selfish agenda. I had assumed that merely being in college implied that I was committed to certain moral ethics linked to some mission or unspoken aspiration of higher education. The concentration of intellect is so strong within the forum of a university, it can transform the world simply by employing its intellectual authority in the right direction in the appropriate way. I suppose that the crisis of leadership that prevails in high places pervades also in universities. How else can we explain classes addressed to social problems that continue to get worse for decades right under the watchful, intelligent eye of the university? Perhaps universities are preoccupied with facilitating the welfare and advancement of the status quo, and oiling the economic and social structure to protect and maintain it. Consequently, instead of preparing to mentor youths like yourself who are coming in to refine your sense of purpose for coming to college, they are more likely to take advantage of your energy and enthusiasm to advance the institutions' more ambitious agendas. The politics of that kind of learning environment can reduce even the most sincere and competent into blundering charlatans. Imagine how you can be easily misled, redirected, distracted or even confused with the double signals with which you are bombarded all day and night, when you should be preparing yourself for your single focus. When I had my opportunity, I had no choice but to take the fullest advantage of the privilege lent to me. I can assure you that I could not afford to let college do what it wanted with me. I conferred with my advisors carefully to make certain that I did what I wanted with college. When you approach your college education with that attitude, time is never enough and even graduation is just a phase of your lifelong endeavors.

One of the biggest challenges you will face is how to finance your education, whether you will struggle and debit, or choose to do a mortgage on your education by accepting credit. While you may be attracted to the temporary comfort of using a credit card, the price you pay subsequently will far outweigh the benefits you get in the long term, if you are not very careful. The privilege that you may think you are accessing by resorting to your credit card may leave you circling in a whirlpool of debts that can threaten or even destroy your financial integrity. Where ever there is an opportunity for goodness and happiness, there are always enemies in pleasant disguises waiting to lure you into pitfalls for their benefit. Credit card companies are no better than other loan sharks in this regard. They depend on your inability to pay to make their profits, when they can exploit the financial laws to the limit to reap the benefits from your weaknesses. However, there would be no need for you to be afraid of credit card companies, their agents or the sumptuous easy offers they provide, if you view them constructively within the context of your needs. You can use the options you have at your disposal and exercise the discipline to invest into this false luxury with discretion. Credit cards can be a necessary and irresistible evil, especially at this stage of your life, but again it is up to you and the choices you make will eliminate any power or control they can have over you. You will have no problem if you can determine dollar for dollar what benefit you will get for the credit you had accepted. If you can work out your benefits to be equal or more than the profits of your creditors, then I will feel more confident that you will make good choices. Be very careful, however, that the tendency to accept credit too readily can become a habit that can develop into an addiction. This habit can lure you to find ways to make life easy and put your whole life on a master pay later plan, a huge debt on resources you have not even started to earn, and limitations on a life you have hardly started to live.

COURTSHIP AND MARRIAGE

My son, I am amazed that I have managed to survive this far in my letter and that I have succeeded in extending your patience this much. If your understanding has increased since you have examined my ideas, I trust, that your patience is mixed with enthusiasm. If there is any benefit you can obtain from any new wisdom, whether on your own or what you have gained from college or reading or even from reading my letter, it would all come to nothing eventually if you select the wrong partner in life. There is no manual or magic formula to accurately predict who can be the best partner, how a courtship should be, or how it could be conducted. Your taste is the carbon copy of your unique personality, and the basis on which some people get attracted varies from pure coincidence to the deepest mystery. That emotional flulike symptom they call the love bug will eventually infect you, and that is one time, for sure, when you will have to deal with it on your own. If you are not infected already, you will still be able to heed some timely advice and readjust your focus a little. If you are already deeply in love and find that you have absolutely no patience to even examine the topic with a clear head, then it is not your fault. I was a little too late, that is all. If, however, you can awaken from even a drunken state of infatuation long enough to set me free of this last obligation to you, I will gladly fade into the background and retire into my world.

I would like to assure you that I did not link those two concepts, courtship and marriage, by accident. In my opinion, they are as inseparable as any married couple would like to be. For me it is more pertinent to view courtship as a trial of marriage until the minds of both parties are made up. The courtesies that you would like to extend or that you have extended to your partner are the same ones you are obligated to extend for as long as you will be together. After all, that is why you both are enjoying each other's company, because you are fulfilling each other's needs and aspirations in the simple little things you are doing together. You do not have to take notes and compare who is giving more or less or who is better at this or that. You just blend in or merge and have a great time just sitting out in the lawn or walking in the park doing virtually nothing but being together. An occasional dinner or boat ride, concert, or party club can add to the spice of life, but they would make no difference with the excitement you two people reach at the very thought of being together. When you start making elaborate preparation to be with each other, to accommodate each other, and especially to excite and attract each other, then your interaction ceases to be natural or normal and has elevated or degraded to the level of romantic diplomatic relations. Whether the level of the relationship has gone up or down depends on what both of you value most in a life together. If, on the other hand, you both value things differently, you will find that instead of enjoying each other's company, you will be preoccupied with each other's value system, making compromises or comparisons or bartering one thing or another. That courtship is a reflection of what your marriage will certainly be. The more effort you have to put to succeed with the courtship, the more you will have to sacrifice to make the marriage work.

Son, there has been a lot of emphasis on this special person, who appears like magic out of nowhere to descend upon your subconscious in the most dramatic way, leaving you breathless. This happens too, more often than not, to young people like yourself whose adventures into the world has just begun and must be flavored with high doses of fantasy to make them dramatic and exciting. There are indeed partners like those that exist, but they hardly emerge with thunder and lightning, drama and fanfare as you see on television or in the movies. Remember to differentiate between those actions, encounters and behaviors that are directed toward you to have that identical effect. Too many moonlight nights like these are deliberately intended to blind your vision and sense of judgment. This situation puts the other party in charge, and you are knocked out of your senses with infatuation or on your knees in submission. These kinds of overwhelming introductions are nearly always staged to elicit responses to a variety of entrapments that may prove to be dangerously addictive. This is what makes them different from courtships, although courtships too can carry their own types of entrapment. The entrapments of courtship are those designed to elicit commitments for the benefit of one partner at the expense of the other, with the view of having that condition permanent as a way of life. The entrapments, however, are generally more deliberate and aggressive, with a short-term agenda to extract the most benefits in the shortest time possible. There are lots of theories and fantastic notions about what love is or can be, but what is not born out of movies and fairy tales are figments of the imagination of celebrated romance novelists and romantic idiots. This notion of two people being born exclusively for each other and destined to go through this world and the next together is enticing enough for any couple to want to believe. All these clutters from myths and necromancies can cloud your perception of your own duties and responsibilities toward your courtship and marriage to keep it alive in a state of constant renewal. During courtship, my strategy, for example, was to get closer to the mother to get an indication of what the daughter would be like. You have to develop your own strategy for your own survival, always remembering that no strategy is foolproof. Keep searching for answers, but keep your partner involved for the adventure so that both of you can share the prize.

It must be in your very best interest that this very special person earns her credentials from merit and not purely from good looks and dramatic social encounters. Personal integrity may be difficult to access very early, but you can begin to get clues from her family, friends, and very close acquaintances. If you even get a hint that her family is involved in any shady criminal underground activity, the late train may be too late for you. Do not be persuaded that a girl is peculiarly different from her family and the type of friends she keeps. If your partner's priority implies that she is playing hide-and-seek to find your weaknesses and shortcomings so that she can prove herself superior or better endowed, you can easily project having her as a mother of your offspring and the kinds of lessons she is likely to teach them. Take note also that someone who cherishes high aspirations and dreams based on sound moral and ethical standards in a conscientious effort to serve humanity does not automatically qualify to be a good partner. She may be an excellent friend or partner in business, but a partner for life as a wife needs that additional crucial credential. That is, of course, the willingness to share those goals with you as an equal partner and team up with you to find ways in which you can embrace each other's future plans. That is a tall order that involves giving up half of one's independence to undertake a responsibility. Very eligible bachelorettes find this extremely difficult, but this can be a good sign that they are worth pursuing. You do not necessarily have to lower your expectations to have easier prospects from which to choose. You need a partner who is a tough lieutenant and copilot to cover your blind spots in life and hold everything together when times are rough and you may be down on your knees. You need a partner who, with all her tenacity, knows how to play and laugh and make any time spent together enjoyable and memorable. If you have not found that partner, son, keep searching until you find one. You do not necessarily have to advertise, ring a bell on the rooftop, or announce it in church. You, your deportment, your pursuit, and your dreams that radiate from you will be the magnet and the shining light that a good woman will not be able to resist. You too will see her taking her place beside you long before the conversation even begins, when, after all the hustle and bustle of the screaming, maddening crowd shopping for prospects, she will be the only one left willing, anxious, and able to tolerate you.

Son, this is one of the first decisions in life you will have to make and get things right in order to survive. The distraction you can suffer from a poor decision can derail you from all your dreams and aspirations, distract you from your lifelong mission and career and eventually your own self. A man who has lost or forgotten his dream, regardless of how strong and powerful he is, is no more than a blindfolded puppet on a noose fumbling on his way through life. I suspect you are thinking that a worthy emotion as love is not supposed to be associated with such destruction, but, son, in the real world love is both the most deadly and uplifting of emotions. It is like fire, both good and bad, depending on who uses it and the use to which it is directed. Love is the fire of all human emotions that must be curtailed and applied to good use, or it can burn out of control. It is ironic that the most powerful force on earth, not the atomic bomb or the nuclear bomb, but love, exists in the hearts and minds of human beings. All the other human emotions, including hate, envy, jealousy, greed, and pride, cannot withstand the force of love. It can be a tool or a magic potion as determined by its user. It is the ultimate omnipotent lethal force contained in hidden vials in our brains. It is this same force that, when combined with others of like minds, can motivate a nation or an empire to act with fire and vehemence. It is the same force that can paralyze your body and your will, move you to abandon your dream, your life's mission, your career, and yourself, just to fulfill its hypnotic demand to obey and be with the object of your desire. It is this same force that, when out of control within you, can explode, it seems, with the force of an atomic bomb and tear your mind and body to shreds, along with all your dreams, your aspirations, and your pride. What makes it even more lethal is that it is very pervasive and can plant its warhead among the forces of hate, envy, jealousy, greed, and pride, some of its deadliest enemies.

This most powerful of all emotions lies quietly and innocently within you waiting like a fire or sleeping tiger to be of service at its master's command. You most certainly would have had encounters with other emotions such as anger and jealousy associated with it, even as a child under circumstances involving your mother, your pet, a close friend or even a toy, but these were merely introductory experiences in preparation for the real thing to come. Son, it is not safe to conduct experiments or play games with the most powerful fire of all human emotions. It will always be a mystery as to whether we have control over how that fire is lit and we fall hopelessly in love. We owe it to ourselves at least to be informed about its nature and potential so that we can make the right decisions before we are consumed by it. If you value yourself and all you live for, you will want to invest or connect it with this most powerful force called love, and, of course, in the right way. A welder does not turn the flames of a propane tank toward himself but toward the purpose for which it is intended to weld or bind two pieces of steel. He will not use it on wood or plastic or paper or any other material for that matter. When life brings you to the crossroad with this special someone, and the atmosphere begins to radiate with heat from that fire which only you both can recognize, you must realize that a powerful alliance between two worlds is about to be formed that can become a blessing or a curse to each other and the world. The fire that you possess can be the most powerful, propelling force to shape your destiny and take you to the heights in the fulfillment of your dreams. Similar to welders with a plan, you can seal your intentions with a will of steel and proceed to build an empire from your dreams, to leave a lasting legacy to be cherished by your offspring and the world. On the other hand, you can test your power and potentials on each other and play fencing games with the fire of love, through ignorance or total surrender to one or more vices of the body or mind, for the entertainment of friends and family, and the world, of course. That is what it means, son, when you meet what you suspect is that special someone, and you tell each other that you are in love.

Furthermore, it is not what you say but what you do that matters. You cannot substitute wood or plastic or paper to be welded for steel. How can you build dreams with materials that are substandard? A conversation or two will give you signals, if you are not captivated by her starry eyes or enticing physique or just blatantly not paying attention. A partner that has no dreams or mission of her own will always feel threatened by yours and will be overcome with envy and jealousy around you. Observe a braggart and egocentric attention seeker, how she speaks, dresses, and behaves, and you can write the history of your life with her even before it has started. The same also goes for you. Like everything else, son, love has its politics that you cannot afford to ignore; just as marriage has its entrapments you will have to endure. If you think I can offer you any further advice or guidance in this direction, I am sorry that I will have to disappoint you. All else I can impart to you is imprinted on you already through the outcome of my own marriage. Be very careful not to let the lessons you extract from our lives be based only on your response to the mistakes your mother and I have made. There are other aspects of our lives that can prove to be invaluable to you in your future decisions and endeavors. Use every occasion and experience as an open book to inform yourself on the path you choose to take in your life. The world out there is an open library always ready to accommodate your research. Do not waste your life and precious resources in endless perambulations to justify who was right or wrong in your parents' marriage. You have to choose your path in life and charter your own destiny the same way we had the opportunity to do ours. This is your opportunity to do yours, with my blessing.

Ten Commandments for Lovers

(written when I was seventeen years old in high school)

1. You may be friendly with other people besides your lover, but you must have no other lover besides your lover, or encourage any secret relations with anyone to whom you are particularly attracted.

2. You must not use the name of love in vain, for your lover will not continue to hold your love in high esteem if you use it as an excuse to satisfy your childish whims and fancies.

3. You must have other interests besides lovemaking.

4. You must not barter your love for a moment's pleasure or satisfaction.

5. Honor your lover and show respect to all his or her acquaintances or anything that belongs to your lover.

6. Be sure to let your lover realize that you recognize and are grateful for every effort your lover is making to make you happy.

7. Avoid nagging altogether.

8. Avoid negative criticism that puts down your lover.

9. Remember to be dutiful and punctual in all your assignments and appointments with your lover.

10. Learn to pretend until the time is right. When things are dark and weary, when you are in a bad mood, when you are jealous or suspicious, learn to smile and pretend.

Rules of Courtship

1. Take note of how you met

There is the belief that nothing in this life happens by chance, and the meeting of two persons is the reuniting of two departed souls. Mysterious and melodramatic as that may sound, you may be inclined to believe anything to explain the coincidence of your meeting. Try not to get too superstitious and philosophical though, and explain the phenomenon to yourself in realistic terms. Where were you both going that your paths crossed? It may not have been as accidental as it may seem. If either or both of you had not conspired to create this encounter and then pretend you did not know about it, that again is another food for thought. It is possible that family members and friends might have been active behind the scenes and are anxious spectators waiting for the outcome. Could it be that by your personalities you share the same goals and were pursuing the same interest in the place that you met? If either of you had devised a plan to go searching, are you certain that you had not grabbed at the first catch and let the rest of the crowd go by unnoticed? Sometimes in your need for a companion, in your fantasy from your dreams, you attach meanings to persons, occasions, and things that do not really exist. In romance, you are often suspended between reality and fantasy and can make believe to yourself that what you see is real. You may resolve in your mind to make what you believe a reality and seek to attach that reality to the first dramatic encounter you have. Take note, however, that she may also be doing the same as you, and you may just be a pawn in her schemes or the fulfillment of her fantasy. Sometimes it is a mystery indeed how and why a human being would catch the eye of another from the far end of a crowd when that person is hardly recognizable, and still decide to pursue the quest to meet. We all are awakened to our dreamland one special day when our eyes and mind seemed to be seeing beyond our normal or usual selves, and we see someone we were hoping or longing to see, to pursue our quest for love and fulfillment in our lives. Well, son, thoughts when strong enough can fly and create the heaven that we seek and bring angels to walk on earth before us. Anyone can become what we make them out to be, not only through our dreams, but also in reality. Two people, however, can dream and make that dream come true only when they do so together.

However, beware of the person who sweeps you off your feet in a sudden rush encounter that leaves you breathless and confused. If it is too good to be true, then create a space of time between you to catch your breath and think things over. You may possibly have been targeted for some unknown reason that may not be for your best health, physical or emotional.

2. Court a person and not an image

Perhaps it is natural for us when we reach adolescence to begin to have fantasies of our dream mate. It is also true that some of these notions of what a dream looks like are fed to us from childhood. Barbie dolls and the other female superheroes were courting our fancy all our youth growing up, and now we can begin to explore the pinups of the adult world. We see them in the movies, on television, on hundreds of magazines, and finally, of course, in our heads. Could you imagine how easy it is to float away into a mind-set of creating a Barbie doll of our own? The girl to whom you are talking is a real person pursuing a dream to better herself and has her own fantasies also of you being a Prince Charming who will marry her and save her from poverty and the curse of being an old maid. When you are young, you tend to go through this ritual of connecting reality with fantasy. Some of us go through the phase of having grand illusions longer than others and tend to do it with everything we do. We spend all our money impulsively on one thing and still want to try the others. We exhaust our energy partying until daylight when we have a written examination to take. It happens to girls too, you must imagine. If both of you are swept off your feet because of each other's strong resemblance to your heroes or fantasy, go ahead and follow through with the fantasy and admire your make-believe doll for what she is not, and she will do the same with you. It would be so very tragic for you to be doing it without the knowledge and consent of the other. It would be even worse if both of you are doing so without each other knowing because of the emotional fallout that can occur after you awaken from your dreams. My advice to you is if you are still obsessed with the fantasy of a Barbie doll or a pinup, seek to deal with and grow past it before you decide to date a girl seriously. Some girls will be either terrified or disappointed at being viewed that way, and others may be even more wary of the consequences. To continue to gloat over a resemblance is to deliberately look past the person herself for all her true qualities which are hers and hers alone. If she recognizes that you are continuing to ignore her, she could take it as an insult instead of a compliment and avoid you for the rest of her life.

There is more to a person than just what you see on the outside. All girls are endowed with externals features worthy of your attention and some are obviously more endowed than others. What you need to do is look beyond the external features of her physical characteristics to the internal of her personality and what she is doing to polish that diamond in the rough within her. What make us different as humans are not only our physical features, but the philosophy we have chosen to determine our destiny. Early in our lives we may temporarily adopt the philosophy of someone who has impressed us, but eventually we readjust and use only elements of other philosophies to shape our own. The philosophy a person has chosen determines the perspective from which he or she views life, interprets and responds to all experiences. What the person reveals from the inside is a more accurate picture than what a person is on the outside. Beauty and charm is more than skin deep. The more you are able to apply this principle to your own life and strive to refine your own philosophy and personality, the better you will be able to look beyond the outer characteristics of the person to the person that radiates within.

3. Avoid a person whose immediate and extended family has a criminal background

She may portray all the qualities of an angel and may even talk and think like one. When you hear how she reasons, you may be even more convinced that she is one. Then you learn eventually about her immediate and extended families and realize that they were involved in criminal activities. She may be innocent and may continue to be for the rest of her life, but her connections to those criminal elements may affect you more than it affects her. The old saying goes that when you marry a girl, you marry the family. There may exist in that family a culture and mentality that you will not be privy to know until you have crossed the line in marriage. All the women in that family already know what that culture is, with its hidden rituals and unspoken vocabulary, and live it on a daily basis. The family may view your courting her as an application to participate in a culture that already exists. To do so as a male would mean to have to be accepted by the male community who are governed by a different set of rules. That would mean to prove yourself and going through a period of probation. As you may observe, I have gone too far into my explanation already. Your romance is already overshadowed and consumed with the idiosyncrasies of this culture. If you have already reached the gate, say goodbye without opening it to enter, before it is too late. I say this because to open that gate is to go into a one-way street for the rest of your life. You will have entered into a Pandora's Box of mysteries and intrigues that you will spend the rest of your life trying to solve. It may not be as bad as I described it, but it may not be worth it risking your romance and your life to find out. The same goes for a girl who is equally a mystery by herself. She seems to be more bent on getting as much information as she could about you, but her connections are all vague or nonexistent. She neither tells you all those stories about herself that can explain her background, nor does she give any clues to the truth of what she is telling you. She dresses expensively but earns minimum wage. She can tell you about family members, but she does not allow you to access information to any one of them. Nothing she says can be verified, yet she talks about it all the time. Take my advice, son, and allow this one to do what she has always done, move on. You will be lucky if she did not get enough information to use against you. These are the types that count their victims like trophies. Try not to become a trophy in the name of love.

4.   Give what you expect

The wise saying that you should do unto others what you would like done unto you, applies equally to courting as well. There are implied obligations, often unspoken, that drive any relationship. Seasonal and birthday gifts are obvious and candid beginnings that may not prove to be as convincing as the little things that prove your deeper concern for the person. You would not be able to help yourself, for instance, admiring a woman who postpones a movie date to allow you some extra study time for an upcoming examination. You should likewise seek opportunities to invest in her future success and peace of mind. The present may portray its fashions, noises, and moments with friends, but behind it all are the tranquil moments she prefers to spend with you, to say nothing but just to feel your presence and your warmth, to bring the world to a standstill to pay homage to the two of you. That ritual can play out in many ways, at any time and place, with codes only you two can read, and not even your best friends can understand. You may ask for clues and she will give them to you, and she will ask because she wants to get better at reading you too. In all that you do, remember that courtship is not a game to win or lose. You are not in a relationship to prove you are good or better or even worthy of her love. Those are higher levels of concerns that will take care of themselves, by themselves. You are there to relate to each other's needs first and to find ways to share responsibilities of fulfilling those needs. You are not there to make an exhibition of your loyalty or sincerity. What you both need is that silent but solid assurance that you are committed to looking out for the health and happiness of each other. After that is firmly realized, all else can fill the void.

5. Do more listening than talking

There is always more clamor in any relationship than what you hear and see on the surface. Similarly, with a woman there is a lot more she is saying than what she is actually expressing, even with her laughter and tears. If you are patient to wait long enough, she will tell you, though not in words again. Words conveyed through our voices only reveal one layer of meaning of a whole battery of intentions and feelings. By their nature, women are very emotional and therefore may find it very difficult to express their feelings through words alone. When feelings surge, we may be too busy analyzing them, much less to be able to interpret and express them. Some of us get overcome by our feelings before we even recognize what they are. This is why it is better, and safer, to interpret what someone is saying by projecting beyond the word to the intention behind the thoughts. Very often she may not be doing a good job at expressing herself because she is overcome by her emotions and the fear of you getting the wrong message. There is a silence that speaks loud and clear, if you tune your mind to hear it. You can learn afresh to listen with your ears tuned to the heart and mind of the person to whom you are connected in such a way that she need not say a word. The best and most vibrant conversation is conducted in silence when two minds take the stage and perform a grand concert and both parties sit close together and listen with their eyes. Perhaps a tear or two, of joy, may fall when she tries to speak and is again lost for words. Son, you can change or even shape the manner you communicate with your partner by the way you listen to each other. Once you have reached that level together, the doors close slowly behind the two of you, and all other concerns disappear to the outside world, and there would be a little need for even a phone call, discussion, or an argument.

6. Take notice how she cares and for what she cares

A person is best known by the things he or she chooses to love and the manner in which he or she expresses that love. These things may evolve into categories or even dimensions but nevertheless give a clear indication to that person's personality and character. Observe a young child with a favorite toy and the value that is put on every action or place connected with this toy and you will begin to understand what I mean. Things a woman may choose to value may very often not be of interest to you but may hold the keys for the success of your courtship, and later, your marriage. It does not matter whether these things are natural or unnatural, living or nonliving things. They may even be tangible material things or intangible matter of no substance or definition. It may be a house plant or flower, a pet, jewelry, or perfume. Just as a child or young animal experiments in play with objects that are crucial for its future survival, human beings focus on things that are important to them for reasons that are peculiar to them. How they express their attachment or affection is worthy of note for you to anticipate the level of interaction you are likely to have with them, if eventually they become a lifelong partner. Again, there are the little things you cannot afford to ignore, because they speak volumes about a person and the lifestyle they are likely to pursue. How much would it take for a person who loves and cherishes a house plant or a pet to forget to water or feed it to the extent where it gets seriously affected as a result of that gross neglect? Even a nonliving thing that was cherished at one time may tell a similar story if it is trampled underfoot or left dragging in the dust of the garage or closet floor. There are some things that we outgrow and some that we take with us, in our bosoms. There is the complete opposite, where a total lack of discretion can lead to voluntary self-abuse to foster an attachment that is overdone. Why would someone be that attached to a car to descend into a state of depression because the car got scratched in the parking lot? What a person chooses to attach to his or her life and the extent they would go to fulfill that attachment lays bare a road map of a day in the life of that person and the one you are likely to share when he or she becomes a life partner. Courtship is a road test of a quality of life being offered to you, and the choice you have to make is not so much when the car is new, but how reliable it will be when the road gets rough and you encounter the inconsistencies and uncertainties of life.

7. Never touch a woman before she is ready (to touch you)

Sometimes after you have become close and familiar with someone, it becomes easy to forget that that person exists in a world of her own and that regardless of how generously she extends her affection toward you, you are still a visitor, though an honored guest. An honored guest, to remain honorable toward his host, must conduct himself in a circumspect and courteous manner to continue to command that respect. He does not take prerogatives to use her space as he chooses, or he may offend his host. If he does, she may not tell him bluntly for fear of disrespecting him and hurting his feelings. However, she may slowly be losing her composure as her honorable guest continues to invade and trample upon her private world. Even after she has upgraded the relationship and you become her fiancé, your obligation has not lessened but in fact has increased to the status of guardian of honor. That means she has invited you into her world not to visit, but to share. Remember the world into which she invited you is still hers and not yours. Even you as a man would be uncomfortable with that kind of imposition into your life and would not forgive the person who is guilty of it. The words and concept we as men use to interpret our encounters are very different from those of a woman. That is because the priorities and sense of urgency in our world are very different from theirs, if not the complete opposite. During your courtship it is safer and more fulfilling for you to negotiate compromises so that both of you get accustomed to exchanging privileges, not taking or demanding them. Give her the honor to keep her rights to her world, and she will return yours to you. In doing so, you will take the lead to establish a level of communication and interaction that will enrich both your lives during the courtship and perhaps a lifetime to come.

8. Cater for growth

We take for granted that changes are inevitable, yet when it comes to courtship we tend to miss the point very easily. Our bodies are evolving as fast as our minds, every minute and every second, more than we realize. The impact of a courtship may expedite this process even further so that each time you meet, it feels like starting all over. In fact, that is how it is for both you and her. Several dimensions of growth had taken place on the physical, emotional, social, spiritual, and other unmentioned areas of which even both of you are not aware. Your brains and your bodies are responding to your new encounter together with fresh insights and inquiries that had not existed when you last met. Hope and aspirations begin to shape a future, and much of this is speculation on the part of either of you, since you are conjecturing them faster than you communicate them to each other. This level of growth can have serious implications for any relationship, regardless of how compatible it might have seemed in the beginning. Growth is not necessarily holistic unless a person consciously contrived it to be so. With men and women having different temperaments and priorities, it is easy to assume that their indulgences would vary and their areas of growth would be inconsistent, and in some cases, conflicting. It is possible for two persons, whose common interest had originally drawn them together, to find them still together physically and in every other aspects be drifted worlds apart from each other. How much more will you mature within a month or a year that will result in changes not obvious to either of you? Some of these changes and the pattern of growth that result may not be within our control; some we may not even be aware of, since they are influenced by chemical or physiological changes within the body. Your personality and other factors peculiar to you influence the way you respond to experiences and grow up to become a man; similarly, she is going through the same routine with her body and mind and is gracious enough to accommodate you during the process. Your obligation is to exercise patience, understanding and help each other get past the difficult hurdles when conflict arises. It is this kind of sharing and caring that permits you to graduate in each other's world. Since growth is inevitable, it would be a good strategy to practice doing it together with someone who may prove to be your life partner one day. That way, you will both have a good head start together.

9. Get practice in trading compromises

If, from our discussion, you can recognize the different worlds in which you and your partner exist, you will understand how and why conflict and differences arise with almost every encounter. It is just a matter of the perspectives being different from which you are viewing the same thing. How about changing the perspective in which you view each other's perspective and that problem will probably solve itself. There is a huge advantage in getting the opportunity to view your world through the eyes of someone else. When you do that wholeheartedly with a partner and dear friend, both of you enjoy the best of both worlds. Your respect for each other and understanding of each other's differences will enable you to interpret conflicts from a unique perspective to the extent where you are able to approach them as adventures. It can be such a great relief when one partner does not have to stumble to find ways to hide his or her shortcomings or be confronted with his or her limitations. Even the deadliest weapons can become toys in a war of compromises. It can be such great fun for two partners to find ways to entertain each other positively by playing social games purely for the fun of it. The more we laugh at ourselves, the better we are likely to acknowledge our faults and correct them. The best person to share that laugh with is a partner, who is close enough to your world to be able to help offer suggestions and even assist you in your efforts. In this imperfect human world of inconsistencies and conflicts, you can do with a safe haven in your life, a person you can trust to give you the best advice and support. That person you will also have to represent in an unending cycle of adventures in the compromises you will always have to make in the many uncertainties of life.

10. If it does not work out, bless her

It may be that your coordination was a little off for the adventures you chose, or the person may have become distracted or disillusioned by imposing circumstances. A relationship is like a dance that two partners are obligated to do and take care of every step they take along the way. If the dancers trip and fall trying to do a difficult step, they take care of each other and start to dance again. However, one or both of them may decide to try that same dance with a different partner. It does not mean that either one was not a good dancer or that the music was bad. It may simply mean that both dancers found out that their talents would be brought out better with another partner. Both dancers therefore thank each other for the time and bow out gracefully from the dance still as friends, with great admiration for each other. A courtship assumes its value through the attitude and the integrity of its partners who bestow their blessings and thank each other for a time well spent. They had paid a visit to another world and now returned to theirs. It is unbecoming and of poor character, as a guest or host, to disclose what were the strong or weak points of either world, or what features there were at all, for the rest of the world to see or hear. How you deal with your courtship, your privacy and that of your partner, especially after it ends, is a reflection of your character and your integrity as a man. If you view your courtship from the correct perspective, it is not supposed to hurt, if and when it ends, although some of them will do. A courtship, regardless of outcome, should be a refreshing, uplifting experience, as each partner exits each other's world a better person than the one who had entered it.

CHOICE OF PARTNER IN LIFE

My son, I wish for your sake that there was a system of arranged marriage so that the choice of a life partner who will share your destiny and bear and raise your children is not based on some fickle encounter with infatuation from the emotional swings of last stages of playful adolescence. I know that was one of the most important decisions I had to make and did not know I needed more time and good advice before I made it. However, left on my own for so long without the constraints and wise guidance of two parents about the true meaning and purpose of life and living, I had taken upon myself the authority to make them. When my mother realized that I had decided to go beyond courtship and marry your mother, she became alarmed and tried to persuade me to delay or postpone my decision altogether. She encouraged several relatives to approach me. I guess I could or should have listened at least, but adolescence is that period of the dark ages of your life where obstinacy, blind brutal self-confidence, and self-conceit are the codes you follow mostly. The more they approached me, the angrier and determined I became to hold my ground and prove myself a man. I viewed the situation from the inside from my newly acquired ego of my early adulthood that it was the first true decision I had been required to make to dictate my own life, and viewed all these relatives as intruders or invaders challenging my newly acquired manhood. Now I can look back and recognize that it was all about me breaking out of a shell in which I felt imprisoned into a world I had created from my imagination. I was not the least aware then that my youthful innocence would be a prey to even very young women looking for victims or scapegoats all under the pretext of love and family. It was beyond my comprehension at that time why a young beautiful girl would commit herself to a long-term relationship with the ulterior motive of exploiting her partner. At that stage of my life I was still too much of an idealist to accept the notion of mothers using their children mainly as pawns to gain legal and financial advantages to support and promote selfish motive to aggrandize themselves at the expense of the child. I did not have the patience to even accommodate any conversation on these topics. For me, life was this phenomenon that I will be able to conquer just like those demons and opponents I had been training to subdue in those martial arts training I gave myself in secret in the dark in my backyard. Your mother was just the trophy or Golden Fleece I was giving myself in advance as my reward. I was proud of myself then, and even now I am convinced that my show of courage and determination was very commendable for my age at that time. My problem with it now is that all that courage was utilized in the wrong way for the wrong reason. I suspect now that the attraction that your mother and I shared was not purely physical, as my relatives emphasized, but emotional also, based on our needs of what was lacking in our lives. She had an absentee father, and I, an absentee mother. My display of courage was the fulfillment of a father image she could then inject into her life, and her submissive, advising adherence to my actions was the perfect complement of a mother image I needed to escape the dead end in my own life and redeem my situation with a family of my own. Both your mother and I wanted to escape the restraints and constraints of our own family situation to launch out on our own to fulfill our dreams. There was no one on either side capable or qualified enough to reach us and persuade us to examine those dreams with ourselves the chief players in it. As you and I can see now, each one of us was an interjector that arrived at the opportune time, and we held on to each other for dear life. Our marriage had been arranged by circumstances, and we did not realize it then. We were too obsessed with the notion that we were taking charge, prompted by the defiant attitude typical of young adults at our age. We fooled ourselves into thinking that we were getting married when in fact we were using each other to marry ourselves. We had locked ourselves into the cage we had designed with our pride, bringing with us the unsorted baggage that we had not dealt with for so long. Your mother was in her late teens and must have felt herself more trapped than I was. We persevered with the realities of our new life as each child expanded new dimensions to our challenges. Even now, however, I believe that the dream was a good one, and we both were worthy of its fulfillment, although the regrets are all we have to share with you today.

Son, if and when you start a serious long-term relationship with that special someone and you both agree to start a family together, you must recognize that you are undertaking your part of the responsibility at a disadvantage. If your partner was raised in a two-parent home, she will recognize your shortcomings and will need to be patient and understanding with you. Some things you will find difficult to understand even after she explains them a hundred times. How you two choose to negotiate your differences will be the key to your success and happiness. Remember one of you has to be the extension of the other in almost every aspect of your lives together and fill in for each other where the shortcoming appears, without making it obvious to the children and, more especially, relatives and friends. There is no need, for example, for it to be broadcast that your wife is not especially good at cooking when you have the skills of a chef. Both of you must control that information, who gets it, when and where, and how it is used. When that information is misused, both of you must deal with the issue accordingly, not because cooking is of such importance, but because little issues like those present excellent opportunities for you to sharpen the tools of loyalty toward the marriage and toward each other. The little things in marriage more often are the synopses of what the big things are and will be. The platforms people construct to perform the act of marriage through life is what narrows their life to the limited dead-end routine that invades almost every aspect of their existence. Marriage is supposed to be a process into the next phase of your life, bringing with it the joys of courtship and the amenities of a tested and tried relationship. The impositions that many couples adopt with the arrival of children are often overdone. These usurp the urgency and importance of the marriage itself. In an attitude of surrender, partners will start saying what they can no longer do because they got married, or that they now have children. That attitude is a recipe for disaster and turmoil that begins to infiltrate and transform from sex to dinnertime conversation, wringing all the moisture and warmth out what used to be and feel like the greatest relationship on earth. Your greatest challenge, son, will be not to get too complacent in your half-orphan mentality, putting yourself on stage to prove to your children and their mother that you can be and do better than what I had done for you. If you find yourself trying that hard, then you are so busy taking the stage fighting your own inner battles, you have no energy left to love and have fun with your wife and kids. You will be present and they will feel as if you are absent. You will be like a ghost scaring them away when they want to get chose to you. Why spend precious moments of this life trying to find ways to introduce yourself to yourself when your children of your own flesh and blood are reaching out to know and love you? Relax and purge yourself of all those zombies of inferiority complex, fear, anger, and loneliness that plagued you in the likeness of me. When you are able to be yourself as your heart wants you to be, you will be more of me than you will ever want to think. It is in the harmony of this cycle that you will recognize your duties even more, to yourself, your wife, your children, and the world. This is the harmony where you must begin, and it is urgent that you find it. We are all part of a big circle in this life that begins somewhere. That somewhere is not a mystery, I can assure you. It begins with you and your partner and extends to each one of your offspring. Not only do you and your partner determine your own destiny by your own thoughts, words, and deeds, but you also influence the destiny of your children. Your circle is linked to others closer to you by relation and by circumstance, and it goes on and on into a huge network linked together infinitely further than you can ever imagine in what we know as the world. Your family circle is like an infinitesimal atom that comprises all matter and intelligence that makes and moves the world. A dead, malfunctioning, diseased circle becomes a sore, a cancer, a cell that can spread its poison up the chain of the network; or you can send the positive electricity of your dream and mission up the network to light up and energize the world with hope, peace, and love. My circle was broken and almost contaminated the world, but yours could heal that wound. Take charge of your circle and connect to the world, and when you do, turn on the lights. When the lights come on, you will find me and I will find you.

SELF-DEFENSE

True self-defense involves a lot more than the physical outward preparation you give yourself in the routine of the various martial arts. Just as there are layers of truth and reality, there are aspects of defense that are not as obvious and are of tremendous importance to your safety and personal security. Self-defense is not so much an art as much as it is a discipline built within or expressed through an art. It matters not what style of self-defense you pursue or use, but the level of discipline you have incorporated into it that will make it effective or worthwhile. Your physical efforts need to connect to the mental to the extent that they become subconsciously adjoined in an adapted way of life, functioning together cohesively and precisely to take command in every situation or circumstance. It involves a different level of conditioning to get the body to respond to what the mind sees or feels. A sense of urgency imposed by danger is one such situation, but if the body had not been conditioned to respond to the solution the mind provides, fear steps in and overtakes you and hinders your access to safety and relief. The mind is an entity with superhuman abilities that needs a body as a tool to work with or through. Its limitations are based on what that body is receptive to explore in shared adventures and challenges of life. The best and most important of these are imaginary that can take you deep into the pits and jungles of fantasy. Yes, son, the body can acquire speed and reflexes faster than the eye can discern only if it is prompted by an equally trained and conditioned mind. When that marriage or cohesion between body and mind is complete, and never really is, you will be able to see without looking, hear without listening, feel without touching, and change position without moving. A weapon or martial arts discipline is just an extension of what the body can accommodate or achieve, but that plane or dimension is extended only by the mind. The only opponent that will present a true challenge is the one who had crossed the border as you did, and you will recognize each other at a glance and come to a truce as brothers.

The best form of defense is a built-in or implied system of prevention. All the elaborate preparations and practice to confront a physical threat when and after it arrives can and may be eliminated. You can maintain an autopilot or radar of identifying and assessing possible threats and intentions long before they find conditions favorable to germinate. Your very lifestyle can be a breeding ground for confrontations resulting from bad sentiments between you and other fellow human beings. I am referring to conditions and circumstances that in themselves harbor the potentials for explosive actions or reactions because of the nature of a person or persons around you. These situations usually start with intentional nonphysical attack on your integrity, ambitions, good will, or even personal possession or talent or other capability that stands out as a threat or affront to less capable or unaccomplished people. All smiles do not bring genuine laughter. A person who asks you, "Who do you think you are," will not rest until he or she has reduced you to what he or she thinks or wants you to be. On your job, there is the disease of professional envy that can spread like an epidemic under weak and manipulative management. Bars and social clubs are not places to stand out too prominently or announce your comings and goings. The extraordinarily dressed lady with all things matching, including her car, may not be that lonely as she makes herself look and may be staging a performance for the convenience of persons you would not like to meet. Even a healthy courting relationship can bring its own surprises of a fatal attraction, a jealous or jilted rival blind and distracted with grief or rage. Beware of those deserted areas, convenient dead ends, and pristine gated neighborhoods where your invitation is either doubtful or questionable, especially after midnight, when everybody else is too comfortable but you. Even among family members there is sibling rivalry and envy that can explode into uncontrollable rage at the wrong time and place. Property inheritance issues can transform even the best of individuals to deadly enemies. These are the most important and crucial aspect of personal defense for which there can be little or no training and preparation. What you do not know can hurt you; and even knowing what you know or what you think you know can be of greater danger to you. The higher your physical training takes you over the top with confidence, the more you are susceptible to spiritual or moral entrapments that lead back to physical pitfalls. The best approach is to keep your spirit pure, your motives and your hands clean of mischief so that you can see clearly and still enjoy a good appetite for life. Still, I would take back some of what I have said about mixing with certain people and being in certain places. The world is crowded with people who maintain double personalities, sustained by criminal minds. There are blue color, white color, and downright ghetto crimes. Some people maintain a grand lifestyle living on the fringe of good and evil. To really know them, you have to be with them, associate with them, pretend to be one of them. Walking this tight rope is a precarious gamble, but it is worth it in the long run, provided you know how to use the information you gained to good uses. Exposing them would be just as bad politics as blackmailing them for profit or self-aggrandizement. When you arrive eventually at the top of the hill of enlightenment, harmony, and discretion, you will be able to understand that the sea of humanity operates in waves and phases, trading places according to circumstances, and flowing with the moon and the stars and the idolatry of their worship. You will have learned how difficult it is to differentiate between lawmakers and lawbreakers, policemen and bandits, priests and perverts, ladies and courtesans, wives and prostitutes. The list can go on and on indefinitely, and it will and does not matter to you. You will have the eyes to see and mind to know.

The Ten Commandments of Self-Defense

1. WALK DEFENSE. Foresee the situation and avoid it. It is not enough to blame someone, lament the misfortune or the unpleasant encounter. To some extent you were responsible for being there, for becoming a target and the nurturing of it to that level. The girl for whom you are about to fight may not be worth it and may be engineering these games to gain attention. The jealous lover you are about to fight may be her type, and he is about to use you to prove it. Self-defense is proactive but will not respond to aggression by yielding to its temptations. Stay calm and your opponent may be forced to think long enough for you to walk or even run away. You may win the battle, but you may also lose the war. The retaliations, the police investigations, the cost of having to prove yourself acting purely in self-defense, the guilt of having hurt someone are all not worth the victory. Call a truce and negotiate for a settlement. Help your opponent find a basis for one.

2. THINK DEFENSE. Do not underestimate any opponent's ability. Never turn your back unless you are in a comfortable position of high alert. A shrewd opponent is not necessarily beaten because he is down or even out. He may be luring you into the trap of feeling overly confident to weaken your resolve only to run you over in the end. The most seemingly weak and helpless person has the hidden capacity to make up for his or her deficiencies. It is a built-in mechanism with all living organisms. Human beings have the ability to train and develop their hidden potentials and keep their secret. Try not to be a victim of this lack of foresight. Keep your mind focused on the opponent's strength, not his weaknesses. A smart opponent may even put on an act of poor performance to set you up for a real attack.

3. DEMORALIZE. Lock yourself into your opponent. A battle is first executed mentally and psychologically. Stare him down, talk to him through your eyes, and let his brain keep busy warding off your thoughts. If you can break his willpower, his morale will crumble, and he would not have much mental composure to engage in an intense battle. In this way, a battle is lost or won long before it is started. Look into his eyes, not at his terrible hands or feet, or the stance he has taken. Rather, read into his mind to assess what he is trying to do so that you can distract him and counter his moves. Distract him to the point of

frustration without even hitting him, and panic will overcome him. He will begin to get confused and desperate but keep his eyes locked in as you generate strong thoughts of confidence on your part into his mind. Avoid a head-on clash, especially when your opponent is overcome with panic and desperation. Fear is the key that can unlock his hidden potential, and it can come spilling out with more than you can control. Your aim is disarm him from finding those potentials by keeping his mind preoccupied with an endless stream of prerequisites that you are presenting before him. Hurt the opponent's pride and he will be halfway down to his knees before you.

4. STAY FOCUSED. Do not follow your opponent, lead him. When he tries to dictate the pace and nature of the fight, use crafty defense tactics to defend and evade so that he realizes that you have just ignored them and that his efforts are of no consequence to you. When he rushes you, secure yourself and rebuff his advances. Never let him see you step backward or spit blood. ; Sting him with a leading jab or a hook or with a flurry that leaves him so confused that he forgets what he was trying to do. Counter him with opposites to his style or intention. If he rushes you for a head-on clash, counter with evasion techniques and let him fall over himself trying to find you. Change your attack and defense procedure so regularly, that he will be busy trying to read into your tactics than fighting his own fight. In all you do, remain calm and show that you are in charge and that, where you are concerned, the fight has not even begun. Meanwhile, he must feel so restricted by your presence that he cannot breathe.

5. TAKE THE LEAD. The best form of defense is attack. In every aspect of a battle, be the one to take the lead. Even your defense moves must incorporate a counterattack in one smooth and decisive motion. Unless expertly trained in such reflex responses, your opponent will be totally unprepared for a countermove in the middle of his attack. Such blows penetrate deeper than usual and leaves the opponent breathless and in sheer agony. A weapon is just an extension of the man. The more you focus on the opponent, the less he will be able to focus on his weapons or tactics and the more demoralized and helpless he will become.

6. ECONOMIZE. Do not waste energy. Do not punch when it will not materialize into a blow. Do not make fancy moves to look good to

onlookers, to impress anyone or fool your opponent. Leave that for your opponent to do, while you aim for every muscle, every joint, and every bone and nerve center. Concentrate on targets with precise timing, pressure, and purpose. You may, for example, slap or jab to distract as you follow up with a grinding hook to midsection for serious punishment. Evade a deadly punch and never get emotionally involved with what your opponent says or does during a fight. When you are demolishing him, just cruise toward the next phase.

7. STRATEGIZE. Keep your intentions secret; they are your secret weapons, and no one has a right to even see where they are hidden much less know what they are. To telegraph your punches is to tell your opponent to prepare for it and put up his guard to avoid you hurting him. This only happens among sparring partners and friends. In a short while your opponent will be exposed to your whole arsenal of tricks and take you for granted and beat the daylight out of you. Keep your most deadly punches for last, even if you never had cause to use them. There may be a return bout or even two, when it may become necessary to use them then. Better still, apply your most deadly blows when your opponent is in motion and cannot read them and has to be told about them by an onlooker. When you apply your deadly tricks, your opponent must not know what hit him.

8. CONCEPTUALIZE. Imagine the battle in your mind. Keep your mind and vision clear. Focus all your attention and energy on your strategy. Try not to get upset and angry because your opponent scored a hit or two. Do not let your pride get the upper hand and force you into a defensive position. Even if your opponent scores a few victory shots, let him see you smile as if you acknowledge him for his achievements. Do it just to clear your mind and distract your opponents into wondering about your strange and unexpected reaction. Force him to adopt what is supposed to be your dilemma. He gets distracted instead of you. He is the one who gets angry and frustrated when you score on him because he is not as attentive as he is supposed to be. Once you succeed in breaking his rhythm, keep on the pressure with little antics or gestures and foot movements that have no meaning. Force him to pay attention by incorporating these movements into an attack procedure so that he has to figure out how it is done. Be very careful not to get distracted yourself by what you are doing and suffer great humiliation for fooling

around. Keep all emotions and distractions at bay, before, during, and after a fight. See nothing, feel nothing, hear nothing but what concerns you before your eyes.

9. CAPITALIZE. Conclude each cycle of attack with precision, speed, and power. When you have to strike, make it quick and deadly. Waste no time in acrobatic maneuvers and stylistic postures. Those are only good for exhibitions. You should already have a menu of deadly combinations from which to choose; apply them as you see fit. If you had been training as you should, your body reflexes will make the selections for you. Your first serious attack will destroy the morale of your opponents since fear, confusion, and panic will paralyze their fighting mechanisms. Every strike from you must be petrifying, bone crushing, and impossible to decode. What must undo your opponent is his inability to assess how he was hit by blows that demobilize his entire body. Your main objective is to punish his spirit first and the body will respond accordingly. It will beg to surrender although its owner will still be putting up a show to save face. By being deadly I mean that your blows must have the quality of execution to make them appear and feel deadly. You need not make them so, unless your life is seriously threatened, but when you mean business, you must resemble a harbinger of destruction and terror. Counterattack along the channel and the source of your opponent's attack while that action is in motion, for therein is the open door of your opponent's defense. Strike fast and sure, before the door of opportunity closes on you.

10. GET BACK TO NORMAL. Take the lead in bringing the struggle to an end. Shake your opponent's hand and compliment him for giving a fair fight. Tell him he is a good fighter and make him feel he could have won too and how much you regret that you both had to match your skills under those negative circumstances instead of doing it as friends. If he is still hurting, offer to call an ambulance to take him to a hospital. Call him at home a day or two later to find out about his pain, or if the injury is healed. If he looks open and ready for it, ask him to forgive you what you had done to him and that you never had it in your mind to injure him in the first place. Your greatest victory would be to get him to yield and reach an amicable compromise with you. If your opponent is smart, he will come to admire you for your efforts and want to be your friend.

Noncombat Self-Defense for Life

1. Keep practicing the katas of life. Exercise your body and mind in a regular routine. Let both body and mind expect it.

2. Set aside special time to be alone with yourself to commune with your body and soul. They may be waiting to alert you about physical and spiritual enemies even you may be harboring right at your gate.

3. Learn to love. Find someone to cherish and win his or her love in return. An enemy is a most valuable trophy to win to your side.

4. Learn something new every day about an unfamiliar topic or area of study; also, add something new to your familiar area of study.

5. Feed yourself and not let someone else feed you, but be careful to examine everything you are about to ingest into your body and mind. The first batch may be good, but the second may be the potent dose.

6. Equalize yourself. Stay low key. Most people cannot tolerate anyone being better than they are, and you may become a source of torture to them.

7. Tolerate but do not accommodate people who are not your type. A talebearer, a gossipmonger, a loud person of loose character is perpetually seeking new recruits of quality personnel to give some credibility to his or her low motives.

8. Do not lend of yourself or your resources. What you can afford, give and forget it.

9. Change your position. Do not become a fossil in your job, your position, on an issue, or the ideas you harbor in your mind. The ultimate law of nature is change.

10. Know your limitations and give the Supreme Being all the glory. Be aware that in spite of all you are, have become or will be, you will reach your peak; and hover for a while; then you head downhill to make way for the next phase, and the next generation of which you can hardly be a part. Be gracious, then, to bow out with a smile.

11. Be a soldier in life. Do what you can to help the wounded, the bereaved, the displaced, and the dead. Bury what has to be buried, put on your helmet of resolve, and move on. Do not stand weeping to inhale the philosophy of the dead. The plague affects the living, not the dead.

12. Avoid clutter in your life of people, ideas, and things. Keep yourself slim, shed and trim. You do not need an overcrowded wardrobe, four cars that need parking, or a crowd of loud beer lickers at your house every evening and weekend.

How to Prepare for Success

1. Think like a king, but work like a slave: be the slave and master all in one.

2. Know your territory and the prevailing king in the open field. Acquire the skills you need to greet your opponent as a competitor, not as a mere rival.

3. Reason with masters: read a good book every day.

4. Specialize in skills suited to your capabilities and drive.

5. The road to success is a lonely one: Don't expect or count on a partner or friend.

6. Avoid the wide highway: cut your own tracks.

7. Do not share your provisions with other hikers: after you cross tracks with other hikers, keep an eye around you.

8. Do not slack up or celebrate until you brace the tape: stay in your own lane.

9. Have reserved plans and provisions for unexpected demands.

10. Remember, success is beginning of a new level and a new journey.

Dare To Be Lonely

1. Never let yourself feel inadequate for being alone. You have all rights to be alone when you are pursuing high goals and ideals peculiar to only you. An interruption or untimely intervention can be a gross provocation and prove fatal to your dreams.

2. Learn to live with yourself first. Keep busy polishing the rough edges of your personality and learn to converse with your inner being. You will be surprised to know that the sage in you is as sophisticated as any other that stunned the world.

3. When people laugh at you, they may actually be trying to cover up on their own inadequacies of being in your presence when your wisdom, ingenuity, and strength begin to play havoc with their feeble minds.

4. Excuse yourself for feeling lonely. It is natural for man or woman was not born to live alone. It is, however, abnormal for a person of strong will to focus on feelings of loneliness. It is a sad induction that he or she has reached a state of compromise on his or her ideals in exchange for companionship and social acceptance.

5. Try being a child who sneaks away to create his own dream world under a tree, among some shrubs, or even in a barn or abandoned doghouse; Dare to be alone to etch your own heaven out of ordinary everyday occasions in your life. Take a vacation with yourself. Put on the neon lights within your mind and have a party within your inner sanctuary.

6. The truth is you are never truly alone; there are spiritual forces forever trying to blend themselves into your world. There are two big political parties of the spirit: good and evil, of light and darkness. Your mind pervades both worlds, but the party you choose to support will influence the kinds of thoughts and desires you harbor in your minds. You do not need to publish to which party you belong. Your thoughts will take you there in a flash. When you get peeved about your public status, burdened with lust and temptation of all kinds, yearning for popularity and fame, and exhausted from excruciating efforts to compile wealth

and material possessions, you will experience a tempest in your heart forever raging until your are convinced that your life is worth nothing. When every second is a piece of heaven, and the most tumultuous storms in your life cannot take away that perfect peace in your heart, the light in your eyes and the smile on your face will reveal that you yourself are the source of perfect peace and light.

7. Fill the secret chambers of your mind with powers of goodness and light. Keep it charged and magnetic with higher-order thinking that enriches and rejuvenates the spirit. Enter into communion with the Supreme Being and feed upon the ethers of wisdom as you mediate and experience the true joys of being alone.

ENEMIES

To protect yourself and your interests in the battle of life, you will need to be bifocal and still be able to see behind the masks and flamboyant costumes your enemies wear, or when they choose to transform from one phase of disguise to the next. I know that it is poor comfort to tell you that the major war in which you will be engaged throughout your life will be an illusion going on in your head. The heat of the conflict will be raging long before and after your physical being is involved, and your victory or defeat will depend on how alert, precise, and decisive you are in your response. Son, as I have implied before, you cannot fight or strike what you have not seen: and what you cannot and will not see, you will not be inclined to prepare yourself to fight. The worst form of slumber and negligence is the mental, psychological, and spiritual, one that goes on in your head. It leaves you open for easy picking for all the vicious predators that roam like demons in the dark regions of your mind. The outer physical world and the inner world in your mind are interconnected more than you can imagine and can impact your fate with everlasting effect. If you are to survive in the regions of your mind, you will have to train your mind to be such a formidable factor of defense so that it will be able to subdue and, in some cases, devastate the demons that lurk and roam there.

When I was a young lad like you, I became totally preoccupied with becoming efficient in as many of the martial arts as I could introduce to myself. I did amateur boxing, tae kwon do, karate, judo, and even amateur fencing. I realized I could not fulfill my dream to be fully competent because each of these skills required years of training with qualified instructors and partners to practice. Each required one of my entire lifetime, and that would still make me vulnerable to the other styles I had not reached. Still, I remained dedicated to that pursuit of perfection and invincibility and trained with myself in the darkness for hours into the night. I felt very good doing it, but not as confident that I was reaching my goal, although I was understudying the masters of the various martial arts from almost every film on the screen. My mentor had challenged us to a duel in three months, and we were left on our own to prepare to meet him. His aim was to find out if we could take the principles he taught us to train to become masters of our own. He never wanted to be called a martial artist and worked as an ordinary security guard for meager wages. What I admired most about him was his ability to remain humble and ordinary in his lifestyle while possessing such great power and skill at his fingertips that could have earned him fame and fortune. His philosophy was that every man is obligated to develop his fighting spirit and his own style. That was the greatest and most crucial test of courage I would have faced in my life at the time. I did not have to do it, but if I did not, I would not have been able to live comfortably with myself from then on. He had always been quite a challenge to keep up with, even in training, and would easily make target practice of all of us as if we were toy robots, regardless of how hard we tried to trick him. I trained feverishly, until one day it dawned on me that I was training in the wrong way and in the wrong direction. I realized that our trainer could have beaten us because he had made us the way we were through his training. We were indeed his robots because all we had in our heads were instilled into us by him, and we were using it the way he had given it to us. We were therefore no challenge because we were an extension of him. I suspected that he had become bored of us and challenged us to this duel to bring some new life to his world.

This is how I first got the idea of the battle of illusions. I created a monster in my mind for an opponent, made him as terrible, strong, fast, and deadly as I wanted him to be, and then fought him every night in the dark. Thirty years later, I observed similar characters in your video games, except that your monsters were prefabricated for you, and you fought them on a screen with a control in your hand. I knew I was in the right path to challenging my mentor, and he quickly conceded when we met. He was quick to inquire about my techniques and methods of training, and after I explained them to him, he confessed that he would adopt them for himself. He realized that he no longer needed us for target practice to boost his ego, because he could create his own opponents for target practice for himself. He had learned something from me, his trainee, which was probably to him the most valuable lesson to take with him for the rest of his life. That lesson is not necessarily about winning a battle, which was my original intention, but more about elevating me to the next phase of existence where the deadliest of battles would not disturb my composure. Every night I had gone through the phase of being afraid for a reason and then deliberately and systematically destroying the agent or harbinger of that fear. After so many trials, I was not necessarily fearless, but I was truly not afraid anymore. I was not afraid because the demons I had been fighting in my imaginary battles were far from human. They were gorillas, grizzly bears, ape-men, snakes, and dragons and every combination of terror that was beyond human capabilities.

Son, I am trying to explain to you how that series of events transformed my life and the way I looked at things. First of all I was able to think through issues more clearly that previously tortured me because I would get too emotionally involved with them. I had almost lost the ability to get angry or fearful because I was busy fighting the imaginary opponents I had created and getting myself ready to overcome the fear of them lunging forward in a predatory attack to devour me. I made them real and kept them real until their anger and my fear had gone, and I had conquered them. I fought them, but the battle went on in my head, as I sweated, kicked and performed every move I had adopted from every martial arts movie I had seen. Since I had lost those tendencies to be angry and fearful, I found myself unwilling to engage in or even talk about fighting. When I graduated myself from my self-proclaimed school of imaginary battles, a new person in me emerged that was more calm, focused, and ready for life's challenges. I failed to get into altercations with hot-blooded young warmongers of my time. The sting that they would have inflicted on my emotion before had already been plucked out because of the training I had endured. On one occasion on a dark lonely road, I was confronted by a gang of young men led by a big bully who demanded that I release to him the girl I was escorting. When I unleashed myself onto him, his friends fled in terror leaving him behind to plead for mercy. I could have afforded to forgive him and walk away calmly because he was still not as terrible looking as some of the monsters I had fought. The following day he was struck dumb with surprise when I showed up at his place to encourage him to seek medical attention. We became friends that day. The other me would have lost control and done as much damage to him as was possible and would have been there the following day to finish him off. The other me would have been serving life for a murder charge, been already executed, or killed in a brawl. I saved myself because of those imaginary battles I formulated in my head.

The most important lesson here comes down to what I chose to do with what I had learned. I could have used my new skills like a secret weapon to aggrandize myself in every public place, but even at your age I had higher goals and aspirations. I had to raise the stakes to seek out a more powerful enemy to fight a different fight in the battlefields of my mind. I quickly figured out that the demons that we labor to fight and flee from are manufactured in our minds and given life and limbs in the physical world around us. We humans nurture them and pet them for our convenience and pleasure until they out-serve their purpose and grow too big for us to control. We love to have our little hatcheries and embryo farms of greed and lust and all manners of corruption. Some of us are beyond hatching and harboring demons; we are so overcome by them that we have become the demons ourselves. How I went about fighting that battle would be a mystery you would be able to figure out by yourself if you make the right choices. I could just leave you a hint or two that may lead you on your way. A partner or best friend or associate who has no dreams or mission of his or her own and always inquiring into yours is a potential enemy who can transform into a demon when the timing is right. A most formidable and dangerous enemy is the person who attacks your dreams and aspirations, the very soul your being. They are the most tenacious. All I have labored to explain to you about enemies and demons will not be complete or sincere unless I leave with you one last important fact. The place you must always begin to search for demons is within yourself, your own mind and the desires and wishes you harbor in your heart. You are your worst enemy because it is you who harbor these secret embryos and innocent demonic eggs. It is a part of your human nature, built into your genes waiting to trigger off into action when the circumstances are ripe to hatch them. When other people are the problem, I can and will fight side by side to save the battle of the day, but when you are the harbinger of your own downfall, the manufacturer of your own demons, even I would have to flee for my own safety. Any tendency or desire, fad or fashion, whether physical or mental, emotional or spiritual, that you are unable to analyze, examine, and control within limits is an enemy or potential demon you are nurturing in your own mind as a secret weapon that could turn back to bite you. Remember demons destroy dreams, and a man without a dream has no soul, no direction or true purpose for living. A demon is an enemy for life, and although you do not enjoy the freedom to go through life without it, just make absolutely certain you are not the one to bring it into your life.

Your greatest enemy in this life is your attachment or involvement to anything in the extreme, whether it is good or evil, love or hate in the darkness or in the light. Recognizing and being able to negotiate and implement the checks and balances to circumstance in your public and private life would be the key to your success in the long run. Developing your unique foresight to anticipate pitfalls and opportunities, and designing strategies to exploit them to your advantage is the true meaning of fighting the battle of life. It also means as you battle with opposing circumstances and opponents that you can see, keep your shield ready, and be alert for arrows that come out of nowhere, or circumstances beyond your control that could change everything forever. Many talented and efficient soldiers of this life have been lost to complacency or excess. Striking a good balance, while still being flexible is the key to the success in any venture. There is no guarantee that you are destined to succeed the way you planned your life, or in the direction you decided to go. Guarantees result in complacencies that provide diseases of the mind. Why play a game that you are guaranteed to win anyway? Overconfidence is the pitfall that awaits the rushing of all fools.

There is one crucial advice I must leave with you that is just as important as the rest. You must always remember that you are not alone. There are others of equal strength and tenacity in another part of the circle in the network fighting the same battle as you. They may be in your ranks just next door, across the street, on your job, or in your church. Adopt that person as your brother. Block with your shield that arrow that would have hit him in the back, rescue him if he is surrounded in the deadly fray, and take him to safety and help nurse his wounds. The real test of a man's character is what he does when he is down on his knees and knows how to get back up. In like manner, your real temptation or test of your character will come when you are confronted with the less fortunate, the fallen and the wounded, and those who are victims of their own bad decisions or their repressive and exploitive schemes of others. Of course, some of them by their very nature are entrapments by themselves, but you will have to use your better instinct to select and differentiate when extending your good will and intentions. This is an example of the extreme I referred to earlier.

There are forces alert and ready to exploit your charitable, forgiving, and amiable spirit, who would strike like lightning to ensnare and surround you, even if they have to stage the circumstances to entice you into their den. When evil persons camouflage their disguise to use the principles of good, such as peace and love, to wage war on humanity, you will have no alternative to be quick and decisive. I trust you will do what has to be done, if you can identify or find them. Their greatest strength and fortitude is in their disguise and hiding places. They win your confidence by saying and doing things that win people's trust and become confidants and trustees in high and holy places, as they set up a network of their own. They may even operate alone to target a particular group of people to satisfy a personal vendetta. One of them, son, may even have won your confidence to become your best friend. Arrows that fly in the thick of battle out of nowhere had to come from somewhere. Things are not always as they appear to be.

Please do not be surprised or confused when I ask you for the same consideration and empathy for your enemies as I ask for a fallen comrade. Strike them down if and when you must, but only in self-defense. An enemy is not very much different from anyone else, friend relative or comrade. We all have the potentials to be enemies to others because of that part of our nature that makes us selfish, envious, greedy, or ambitious. All of these vices are virtues that have gone into excess and developed the potential to hurt others and our own selves. The people we view as our enemies are actually very good people too, whose ambitions and aspirations are so different from ours that they choose to achieve their ambitions at our expense or discomfort. Be careful not to assume that your enemy is a particular type of human being who is of a different race, color, or religious conviction or culture or even from a neighborhood which is associated with bad experiences. Avoid these pitfalls of logical thinking from your mind and take a second look at the person or persons who attempt to introduce them on you. Enemies are more or less bred out of circumstances and conditions based on conflict of interest, and parties may choose to settle their differences by trickery or force instead of resolving the differences through negotiations or peaceful means. It happens with nations, societies, organizations, and families. It even happens within families, between brothers and sisters, between husband and wife.

When you are unconsciously an enemy unto yourself, there persists in your mind a perpetual war zone of endless battles still unfought. Similar to veterans returning from a real war and suffering with the aftereffects of post-traumatic stress disorder, in the midst of peace you can envisage destruction and chaos, and even sounds of merriment can trigger the most adverse of reactions within you. Persons who are exposed to prolonged stress and torture suffer from hallucinations that translate into real-life unpredictable behaviors. Fathers and mothers of broken relationships who had already tortured each other with all their will and might and are now normal-looking people on the outside, but their insides are thoroughly scorched and shredded. These two handicapped leftovers are placed in the arena of the court system, closely supervised for accountability and responsibility, one given the sword and the other the shield, to take whatever advantage is available of each other, while the system keeps the scores, in the best interest of the child. This is the war zone of desperation, betrayal, and destruction under which a child is raised, out of what was supposed to be a wholesome family. Yet conscientious advocates, teaming up with social workers, ambitious politicians, lawyers, policemen, and bounty hunters, join in the fray, to seek and hunt their prey. Meanwhile, the child is left to endure the spoils of the battle of separation each day and deprived of the comfort and shelter of a true family. Instead of using resources to help keep families together to prevent this tragedy, the system spends ten times those resources to support incentives that help keep them apart. The results are obvious: fathers with destroyed self-esteem roaming aimlessly with what is left of their thrashed selves and mothers bewildered and lost but arrogant from their victories, living up to grand expectations of honor and redress for the sacrifices that they had made. Out of the smoke, rubble, and chaos comes a child, almost a veteran from a battlefield from birth, looking around desperately for love and stability, and redefining these according to his or her lack of understanding. From the temporary holding cells of foster families, halfway homes, and detention centers comes a new breed of warriors camped out or squatting in ghettos and creating their own laws and government and becoming mothers and fathers. This time they are viewed as outcasts and criminals and are gunned down in the alleyways or herded off to the gallows or to jail. This, my son, is the challenge of your generation. If you truly managed to survive the silent war zone of your own life and can still pull your tattered self together, and if you can still summon the willpower to be your true self, then proceed to make the difference only you can make, in your own unique and special way. Dismiss the hypocrisy of pretending that the sheltered life of a single parent was all that the heaven it was shown to be. Use your disadvantage to your advantage to connect with the plight and the psyche of the disadvantaged. In all you do, do it for the upliftment of humanity and not for self-gratification.

If you are tempted to think that the concept of being an enemy to oneself is far-fetched, I would urge you to give it a second and third thought. I reasoned with you before that most of our battles in this life begin and are fought in our minds or up in our heads spreading down to our hearts. Before you dismiss the lifelong truth about this imaginary battle of life, ask the older people of my generation, and you will realize that they can all be divided into three camps. The first large group of people are completely doubtful, lost and have no idea how their lives took shape the way they did and are always complaining and making excuses for themselves. The second group of older folks are more aware but lack the resolve, willpower, or skills to do what they should do and spend their lives being inconsistent and indecisive in almost everything they do, even sometimes for wholesome or unwholesome reasons. The third group is obviously the more decisive, alert, and proactive group that survives on foresight and ingenuity, calculating and recalculating its next move or strategy. Allow me to make an analogous comparison to the way we think and treat our bodies and the way our bodies react and think about us. When we use our bodies to enjoy ourselves gorging on all kinds of exotic foods and substances and subject it to all kinds of outlandish behaviors and ordeals, our bodies kindly and humbly send us signals through symptoms of pain and other forms of discomfort. The first group of people will rush to the doctor for answers and instant relief and will be satisfied with medication that will mask the symptoms, while they resume their reckless behavior in the same deliberate and careless manner. Nothing will stop them until their damaged bodies give up and a disease strikes and they are laid up at home or in a hospital terminally ill. Our solution to our problem of getting overweight may be right in front of us on the table before it is piled high on our plate. We remain in denial as we age more rapidly than we really are. Instead of thinking about what people think about us, we should be more concerned about what our bodies think of us. Yes, we can be so close but yet so far away from our own selves.

The second group of us would be more careful, priding ourselves in what we eat and wear and how we exercise and treat our bodies. This group enjoys the harmony of body and mind and would have enjoyed a perfect heaven on earth in spite of all the struggles of life if only it had not suffered from a lapse of judgment or discretion and done something harmful to both body and mind. When we break our own code of behavior, our bodies and minds recoil with shock and dismay, and the consequences are more devastating. The consequences can be death. Some are not dead, but they spend the rest of their lives dragging around their dead body parts from the mistakes they had made. Living your life in purgatory, forever trying to compensate for what you had not done is not a wholesome way to live, but at least it is a compromise to slipping into hell. Son, I fit into this category. Through lack of judgment and sentimental idealism, I made decisions in my life, the effects of which plague me to this day. I am also the same one who suspected that something was inconsistent with how my life was going but held on to the last straw of hope and faith in the value of human dignity and trusted the wrong people to live up to their words. Over and over I was wounded by those entrapments of assuming people are what they show themselves to be. I had this weakness of judging people by my standards and realizing the truth too late after the damage has already been done. Now you can see that all the name-calling and all the undignified clutter of bad living that prevailed in your life were the direct results of those decisions and lack of decisive actions afterward. To act wrong and be struck down on the battlefield of life is one thing, but failing to be decisive in your action to recover to your feet is almost an unforgivable sin. It multiplied and compounded my mistake by the numbers of persons with whom I came into contact. When people misinterpret you for what you are not, they themselves become incapacitated and respond to you abnormally, thereby increasing the cycle of confusion and deceit. It is a human tragedy for normal people with good intention to be caught into a dragnet of confusion through another person's life. Yes, son, your decision or action can lead other people astray and spread even more confusion.

Yes, son, you can be your own enemy to the extent that you reproduce malcontents of people all around you. When you fail to examine yourself and your actions carefully, you can become so conceited or egotistic that you are blind or insensitive to the effects you are having on others. Sometimes we put the scales on our eyes because we are enjoying some short-term benefit or pleasure, and human nature being what it is, we want to prolong that pleasure for as long as possible. Our influence can be so strong on others that it can put their entire lives on hold and force them to be scrambling around like caged animals trying to regain their composure and get back to their dreams. The danger of human nature is that we are so inherently selfish that we only recognize it when it backfires on us and our loved ones. Even then our first tendency is to separate from those people we affected and take care of our own. Although it seems to be the most logical thing to do, my son, that would be the most fatal of mistakes. You can hardly take care of or protect your loved ones more than you can take care of the world around them. That would be like isolating them on an island of their own, with the flood of reality waiting to invade their lives, or putting them high up on a pedestal that they are lost forever and would never know how to come down, even to experience the basics to survive.

At that stage, you will be the only antidote. Only you can break the cycle of destruction that is destined to follow. The diseases of one generation are the failings of the generation that went before, practically and figuratively speaking. History and politics abound with vivid examples, but the societal tendency is to aggrandize ourselves with the failings of one at the expense of the other, generally labeled as enemies, and build monument to our self-declared heroes to exhilarate ourselves. If only society would do it differently, we could save the forthcoming generations layers of human tragedies in the world to come. If, however, they do as I am asking you to do, then this disease or virus will not stand a chance of survival, and the ink on this paper and my effort will be well spent. If you survive ridding yourself of this self-afflicting disease, you will learn to protect your loved one from it. You will observe it in your daughter when she is very young, trying to manipulate your love and affection for her to satisfy some petty game or fancy. You will know how to lead her lovingly to higher ideals as she grows past that phase in her life. You will see it in your son too trying to make unreasonable demands of his mother, or you, to have his own way with his world around him. Gently and lovingly, but sometimes firmly, you will have to help them to recognize limits and standards, for their own well-being and that of the future world they will occupy and create. You will recognize by now that as parents we do not own children and their minds, or their future. Our children have just been tentatively loaned to us, and as temporary custodians of their health and welfare, we have our duties to fulfill. There is no such preference in nature as to who is better and for what reason. Both father and mother have their peculiar duties to perform for the complete holistic development of the child. I am mystified that the system would impose itself on the family structure and dictate to mothers and fathers their obligations. A system of this kind produces demons or diseases of the mind, not only among mothers and fathers, but also among children. Can you imagine a society with a social, economic, and legal system that is nothing less than an active machinery that produces men, women, and children who are enemies unto themselves and others? Can you imagine a future of that system working through every home to our courts, our schools, or our jails and recycling into society for final digestion? Can you imagine that atmosphere influencing our politicians and lawmakers, our social service system and its leaders? Son, in the future we may not be able to differentiate between our enemies and our friends. Sooner still, we will not be able to recognize ourselves. Imagine the profile of a mother whose main ambition and focus in life is to garnish the earnings of the father of her child and engineer his every discomfort for the rest of his youthful days, in the interest of the child. Try to speculate, if you could, what it would be like to try to extend your hospitality and love to a child or grandchild, who is groomed and sent as an agent to spy on you and fish for issues to bring you harm. Under these conditions, some children, I must admit, would be better off without parents, and parents would be better off without children.

Enemies are not actually enemies until they become so. You must never view someone as an enemy because he or she had been described or declared so by some person or organization. First see an enemy as a person with a cause, a hurt, a need, or an aspiration, and who can be proactive and alert just as you, and who has been confronted with strong opposition. You do not have to imitate a conflict or a war, spilling blood and debris and ill wills that will take generations to begin to undo. Instead that is an excellent opportunity to negotiate how to share compromises, and establish common grounds of interest on which both sides can agree to work together and set boundaries which each side must never cross. You will be surprised to learn eventually, that an enemy may be a best friend you had not met. Negotiating with your enemies, if and when you locate them, will be a necessary process of living as you charter your way in this life. Do not get too obsessed and preoccupied looking out for one so that your mind gets diseased and you start creating one that is not there, or you end up fighting ghosts of your imagination. Alternatively, you may find within your own ranks, colleagues, and friends, who are deeply invested in the production and provocation of enemies because it suits their causes or will benefit their personal ambitions. That, son, will be your greater enemy, whose terms will be more difficult to negotiate and whose mind will be almost impossible to persuade. One enemy breeds even more enemies. How can you persuade or negotiate with such a person when by his very nature, he is an enemy to himself?

Thank you, son, for tolerating me this far, for now I must let you go. I now feel more relieved that I have fulfilled half of my obligations to you, even if just in my imagination. What you choose to do with all that I have told you is your life's choice based on your free will. When I speak of half my obligations, I mean that I wish I were there to be an example to show you how it is done in my way. However, I was one of those who were wounded along the way, but whose spirit and resolve had not quite broken. I have survived to tell you what I learned from the battle of life and must pass on the baton of this race to you. There are hundreds of sons I could adopt to choose one of them to give this baton, but it would not be a natural gift, or a clean handover. Take this baton from me and run this race for your son, and take care not to get wounded in the race.

THE ENEMY WITHIN

The other great danger of that secret enemy within is how they can roam freely with our permission among our children and loved ones. When we harbor complexes and obsessions, they become the premises under which we frame the perspectives of all the meanings in life and our dealings with other people. Your misinterpretation becomes the morality of their lives and the way in which they view the world. Your weakness, therefore, becomes the strength they assume for themselves. To pass on your complex and shortcomings to your children and grandchildren is definitely the worst legacy a parent can leave a child, yet that is what many parents unconsciously do. So blind are we in our self-assured wisdom and self-conceit, we miss the reality that those under our influence had nothing else to refer to but what we present to them. As a result, they are woefully locked into the tunnel vision into which we brought them. Ignorance will therefore become their wisdom, and darkness will be their light, all because you had not done your own introspective search early in life. Already we are tested with our own nature every phase of our growth. Why would we want to condone or inculcate further imperfections that would render us further vulnerable to be passed on with our genes to our children to grow with them like a fungus to their character? Being a parent or leader involves a lot more than providing for physical and material comforts. In many ways, similar to the animal world, we provide insights into how the world works and where we as humans fit into that cycle, except that as humans, we have the privilege of making a choice of good and evil in almost everything we do. From polar bears to eagles to rats, they are programmed to raise their young ultimately to succeed. For them, there is no room for compromise, or their species will go extinct. We have the intelligence and the capacity to shape our destiny and our human condition to almost the level of perfection beyond our imagination. Parents, however, cannot guide their children beyond the stage where they have reached, and those divided in their opinions on issues, standards, ethics, and personal tastes are further handicapped in doing so. Before or even after you become a parent, it is crucial for you to recognize what your weaknesses and limitations are so that you do not inflict your offspring with your shortcomings. I must concede, son, that life will never be perfect regardless of how much we persevere. Our body is built with and subsists on its own diseases and imperfections. We marry or get a partner to form a team be our mirror and helpmate, and that is why when we feel convinced that we have met such a person, we become self-assured to accept the prospect and the challenge to share our offspring with that person. Son, there is obviously no foolproof method to raise and guide a child, for the circumstances of every family varies like the numbers in a lottery. I am convinced that any parent will be as successful in raising a child in so far as he or she is able to keep an eye on himself or herself. Work through your own misgivings, your intuitions, your sincere introspections, and a unique intelligence will connect you to the child. The child will find you through your inner thoughts and feelings, and you will become one in the daily struggles of life. When you micromanage, over analyze, and curtail the natural tendencies of our children, you stifle their growth and leave them disconnected. The fears you harbor for your children may be those you have not yet conquered within yourself. You may be taking advantage of the arena set for the child to conquer and enjoy to swing the game of life to achieve a make-believe victory for yourself. When you as a parent keep a close eye on yourself, the child will feel the magnet and draw close to follow your precepts and guidance more naturally, or instinctively. There is much from the animal world that concerns us as humans, and there is much that does not. The secret and mystery is to know where and when to strike the balance. A child also needs to exercise its intellectual, moral, and spiritual muscle to follow your lead and not be hooked to a leash with a comforter perpetually plucked in its mouth.

Every parent uses a unique approach to accomplish that balance. Much of what you have heard about parent-child relationships, I am certain, has more to do with the one-sided commitment of the parent being obligated to fulfilling the needs of the child. There is this theory that prevails in the best of circles that a child is not responsible for being born into this world; therefore, it is not obligated to anyone, not even to its parents. The advocacy of most humanist movements are adamant that parents, regardless of their circumstance, be made accountable at all costs for the providence of their children. These theorists and advocates aggrandize themselves on the assumptions that the parents they target are devoid of such inclinations to love and care for their children and should have to be forcibly made to do so. A showing or display of love born out of panic and shame must be mortal torture on a parent who is already stripped of all other aspects of authority for the world to see. We admire animals and other species that display affection and protect their young, yet we seemed unwilling to credit parents with this quality of attachment. Son, there are systems in place that either unwittingly or deliberately prey upon vulnerable parents with such vehemence, they are certain to crush the willpower or the natural tendency of any parent under their scrutiny. There are innocent and conscientious parents who are so preoccupied with avoiding becoming a target that they either put up a false show like robots or go totally astray trying to find ways to escape being under the radar. While some have adopted the plausible philosophy of doing heroically whatever it takes to show that love, some have resorted to crime and prostitution and even subjected themselves to the most hideous exploitation to take proactive measures to express that love in tangible ways. A close friend of mine told me that he would even kill if he has to, to provide for his family and was surprised and disappointed when I disagreed with him. At the time my friend was unemployed and I was not. Obviously, I would arrive at a different conclusion because of circumstances. Why should a parent be subjected to external pressures of scrutiny and suspicions when the parent is internally bound to give of his or her best for the child? My friend's situation is just one of the multitudes of problems families face. The system should be more intimately involved with my friend's family in preventing him from reaching that point of desperation.

Then, son, there is that other dimension of this problem where the child is made to feel obligated to the parent. Among adults, for example, there is this regular occurrence of a couple being unequally yoked in a relationship, where one partner's deep concern and commitment to one is not matched with the callous, selfish, and irresponsible attitude of the other. Well, the same can occur in the case of a child, who, through circumstances or bad orientation, can grow up to be a ruthless, egotistic, and lifelong consumer of other people's good graces and love, without the slightest inclination of giving anything in return. These are the very people who eventually become adults and recycled those same attitudes into relationships and then have children of their own. My son, pray that you are not that unfortunate to get tangled up in a relationship with such a person for a partner. These are the kinds of people who will consume everyone with whom they come into contact to satisfy their every expanding appetite for any or everything from personal attention to material things. There is a great tragedy in the course of this life in getting unequally committed in a relationship with a child. The most foolproof way of doing that is sharing that child in a failed relationship with its mother as the dimension of the problem starts to multiply. In a healthy relationship, a baby is supposed to get as much enjoyment and other benefits as it parents. As the child grows older, the interactions change as parent and child communicate differently in the process of bonding with each other. That bonding process is supposed to stay pure and untampered, clean and healthy in a way that most of us adults with children would easily understand, if we are willing to admit it.

Son, raising a child in a healthy relationship is not as complex as you are made to believe. If the child is enjoying the parent and the parent is enjoying the child, then the formula is that simple and complete. It is when the other impositions and flavors are added that you begin to lose your insights and perspectives. You begin to grapple with complicated and over demanding formulae like those more popularly presented to parents today. Any consideration about a relationship with your child is overshadowed with legal ramification dictating what contact you can or cannot have with your child. You are surrounded by this gang of advocates, supposedly there to help you to care and love your child, but whose priorities are practically to scrutinize and punish you for any shortcomings. The standards of child care they impose on parents are equivalent to doctors of pediatric medicine. The financial and other commitments with which parents are saddled to cater for the well-being of their child are many times over their earnings or their other capabilities. Then there is the social worker with a battery of legal experts and laws waiting on the sidelines with folders and reports to lunge into action to oversee the state's requirement at the detriment of the parent. Life of a parent can be consumed keeping a job and providing the basics for the family. However, a simple incident or action on your part that may be misinterpreted or misunderstood can bring officials racing like hyenas to drag your child out of your hands. After all, these external factors have invaded your relationship with your child and shredded your constitution to bits. You and your child may have very little with which to bond. The child may have learned and found it very tempting to sacrifice you and your love for the many enticing alternatives being offered. First the child will be made to feel that he or she is escaping the discipline associated with moral and other constraints that you as a parent had been imposing to raise a balanced child. Then the child who was the gem of your heart and soul can develop an alliance with all the forces available at his or her disposal to reinterpret all your efforts as proof of abuse and neglect and exact a punishment on you worse than death. The last straw is when the mother takes the lead, and your child gets an excellent education in the art of betrayal. That aspect for the child's experience is never defined as "destroying the welfare of a minor," the term commonly used, or "destroying the welfare of a parent" for that matter. My son, pray never to have to take this dark journey ever in your lifetime, or what may be left of your constitution may leave you too little room to love. The man who has forgotten how to love has forgotten how to live.

LOVE AND WAR

We are by nature learners, constantly storing memories and experiences that have stirred up our emotions. Our motivation to learn or do anything is driven by our sense of urgency for the need of that thing. Create the sense of urgency and our faculty is locked into absorbing as much of that as possible. When that sense of urgency is removed, you just follow the paces until you lose interest altogether. Humans are perpetually involved in high-intensity conflicts in issues of love and war throughout their existence. Love and war are like high-speed trains that travel alongside each other on parallel rails that merge or intercept at junctions in the pathways of our lives. Both are driven by the same engine or emotions, fear and desire, and the same feelings, pain and pleasure. We go to extremes to prepare ourselves for war for fear of the consequences of not being ready, and we promptly use those skills to fortify and solidify our chances to fulfill our desires for love. The absence of tension never really exists. Absolute peace and tranquil love are illusions that infect the minds of the feeble and indolent. It is in the preparations for war that peace is maintained and love blossoms forth like lilies of the field in the freshness of spring. Both love and war are born out of circumstances of mounting tensions that start a fire that can both consume us or make us whole. The true victims of war that are ravaged on the outside are generally dead and gone on to heavenly bliss. The others of us who are left behind continue to prolong the destruction among ourselves at every opportunity we get. Hooked on the addictions of power, there are those who venture out on conquests in every area of public life, waging games of war under the innocent banner of doing politics or social work or even promoting the culture of one's ethnic group. There are politicians and political parties, for example, who prey upon their people's virtues and rape their innocent minds, plundering the harvest of goodwill that had been invested in them. These agents are committed to maintain an atmosphere of strife and division that go beyond the harmless dialogue for the common good of their people. The temptation of political genocide is so strong and overwhelming, supporters are coerced into a crusade in order to partake in seemingly innocent atrocities against targeted factions among their midst. It is tragic when this kind of climate becomes a source of comfort to genuine law-abiding citizens who utilize their valuable resources of time and energy toward activities that are equivalent to ethnic cleansing. All of this, meanwhile, goes on in the height of tranquility and perfect peace in the country.

Love can also bring its lethal mix of traps and temptations. Imagine getting involved in a courting relationship with a partner with a warped imagination who wants to peek deeper into your inner being further than she would ever be willing to invite you into hers. You, on the other hand, may even be overtaken with the inclination to yield past the boundaries of an open invitation based on friendship and get embroiled in a scandal or controversy that shreds your good reputation and hers for life. The war of love gets even more deadly when children are involved because the missiles used to bombard the other side are precious feelings, including love itself, and souls of young children, bursting with an enthusiasm for life. Parents who are now disenchanted lovers resort to using their children's needs to create missiles of Greek fire to hurl at each other in a vendetta of retribution and revenge. So obsessed do they become in their self-aggrandizement that they do not realize that the shrapnel and offshoots of their war games wound their children continually, leaving scars long after their parents are thoroughly exhausted and consumed.

Son, if you were to ask me the most brazen question, as young adults your age usually do, about what you must or should do to satisfy me most now that you are on the right track to a wholesome fulfilling life, my answer would be quick, and I would not have to endure this task of prolonging this letter in a feeble attempt to get to the point. My answer would be that you, my son, should strive to always keep yourself versed and equipped in the arts of love and war. You may ask how can I be so quick to conclude that all the issues and priorities of life be contained in those two elements that are so distant from each other. They only seem so, but they are not. War and love are intimately connected, not only because they boast qualities that are the precise opposite of each other but also because one needs the other to embrace its own qualities to make itself legitimate. To be in love is to commit and align yourself and your entire willpower to the forces and virtues of love against those forces and vicissitudes of war. In other words, to be in love is equivalent to being at war; for it is to the extent that you are conscious or conversant with the elements of war will you be successful in your deliberations in love. The more you are in love, the more you are plagued with negative emotions of jealousy, envy, rage, fear, and grief about every little issue connected to them. For the sake of love, you can find yourself on the complete opposite of the spectrum behaving obsessively in ways completely out of character and often not even be aware of it until after you destroyed the fertile garden of love you so deeply cherished. To be in love with someone is to view that person as your prized treasure for the qualities you envisage that person has, and to declare war simultaneously on any other person who dares to recognize those same qualities in that person and can become a potential rival for the affection or even the attention of the person you desire. A man threatened with the loss of his precious love will be transformed into an uncontrollable demon with superhuman strength and the strongest determination to eliminate the source of his grief and loss. To do so, he will engage in all the arts and disguises of war.

To even begin to negotiate a settlement or compromise, you may find it necessary to match his force with yours. What is worse is that you may actually be an innocent passerby in this unfolding drama of blind jealousy and unchecked obsessive behavior and could be at the risk of losing your life for nothing. That is a situation of war that, if you survive or overcome, will define or remake you for the rest of your life. You will become either a victim or a victor, in a pitiful state of helplessness or the confident state of a warrior.

I am very reluctant to even discuss or associate you with the category of the victim, for obvious reasons, although there are people who become inevitably so, whether they are in love or at war. They are often referred to as victims of circumstances. Well, son, a very small percentage may so well be described, but the vast majority of them are definitely not. We are all victims of circumstances to the extent that we have not contributed, directly or indirectly, to the situation in which we find ourselves. These would include natural disasters, accidents, and cross fires, or even a national or international development over which we had no jurisdiction or control. This will include an occurrence of an epidemic of a disease yet to be analyzed or identified. We are, however, not victims when we have the knowledge or have it available to us to enable us to make the right decisions and to act in our defense. Too many of us are professionally dedicated to being victims to enjoy the psychological and material benefits that these bring. The wheels of public institutions seem to be overhauled and greased to serve as institutions of sympathy and mercy by leaders and politicians who find this strategy an easy pathway to power. The public is being conditioned more and more these days to make decision based on empathy and emotions of pity. Everybody is supporting somebody as a hero, who is drawing sympathy for somebody who is a victim, until we get so much into the habit of crying, we even forget what we are crying about. Professional victims in life are always complaining and placing blame away from themselves toward others. The world always needs to stop spinning to attend to their needs and their whining. They are like physical, spiritual, and emotional vegetables blocking traffic in the highways of life, causing congestion and, in some cases, fatal accidents. What is really tragic is that the true victims of their malcontent behavior often join in the choir to shower them with even more praises and sympathy while these social parasites continue to drain the nation and humanity of its good will and fortitude. While I agree that some of us do make genuine mistakes or find ourselves in the wrong place at the wrong time, it is not a good strategy in life to keep wallowing in the pit of self-pity and regret, when there are viable solutions, alternatives, and resources we can grasp to pull ourselves out of the situations we find ourselves. The prevalence of the victim culture has now become almost a profession and an industry. Can you envisage adjusting to a new world order in which our social services, our education, our legal systems, and our churches adjust to accommodate this invasion of proselytes, contaminating a society with this cancer of lethargy? Son, the result will be more destructive than war can ever bring during this stagnation of peace.

Let us, therefore, adjust our focus from the facades and orchestrations of war and look at the real issues relating to the art itself. First of all I have never been a soldier and would never attempt to rationalize on the intricacies of military training. I am a firm supporter of the draft, where every young man should do his stint to maintain a high quality of disciplined population for national security. Similar to any other profession or vocation, it is how far you inculcate its principles into your lifestyle that counts. Wearing an impressive uniform, participating in parades and expanding your skill through various trainings are great beginnings, but the final measure of what makes you a warrior is what trickles down to your daily life and the decisions you make on how it will shape your character. I have never viewed the notion of war as equivalent to the sensationalized staged drama presented on television and the movies. Once you are alive living among humans you are in a perpetual state of war. We are by nature a very warlike species with a tendency to go to extremes to satisfy our selfish whims and vices; once the slightest possibility exists, we want to overcome our victims and use them to serve our purpose. Immediate gratifications are our greatest temptation, especially when our targets are innocent, docile, and complacent idealists, oblivious of our unholy intentions. You do not have to wait for war to be declared and be drafted to become a warrior. You had the potential to be a warrior from the day you were born, and you assume your status in this life the day you wean yourself from your parents and all the institutions that trained and educated you. A true warrior picks his own battles, not the ones that are picked for him to make him distinguished through the raw abuse of power for the aggrandizement of some leader or politician. There is the war of the degenerate where man and machine clash in a wanton display of raw force to produce mayhem and destruction, and medals are gained and monuments built to select the token heroes out of the desolation and distress left behind. Then there is the war of the uplifted where the clash of wills between good and evil are fought in the domain of the spirit, where an unrelenting battle rages until our last breath is expired. This is the battle of battles that interests me most, where victory is the redemption of your soul. Physical training with deep purposeful insights into possibilities beyond the ordinary human ability and perspectives can earn you temporary invincibility and the self-confidence that come with it. Extend the conventional limits of the training that is available to incorporate into your natural abilities with these preferences and you will have no reason to fear man or beast. The human body when systematically trained and conditioned can reach superhuman levels of performance if you develop the will, capacity, and patience to endure it. The confidence you will have acquired from the superior training you have given yourself will uplift you to the next level of existence where you are the humblest, most peaceful man in the world. I will call this level of existence the domain of extremes where you live on one plane but exist on another. You will be aware of your invincibility and still find it easy to look and behave as harmless and peaceful as a fly.

In this domain you will find that physical battle is unnecessary and that you will have lost the satisfaction of winning one. The insipid efforts of your opponents will disgust you, especially when you are forced to punish them. The true benefit for you, however, is that the harsh training at the physical and emotional level is what conditions your willpower for the equivalent struggle at that spiritual level. Men of limited means and intellect are quick to resort to physical confrontation and weaponry so that they can be seen on stage for that glorious moment. When you are on the domain of extremes you see how the world works. The forces of nature exist in the nature of man in constant maneuver in a war game for superiority and control. When you witness the destruction executed by a morally feeble mind, entrenched on the throne of power in this physical world, you will find your mission again. As you arrive at that plane, with the right training and quality of spirit, you will know what to do. You will, hopefully, see the elements of love in war, and the war in love, the good in the evil, and the evil in the good.

CONCLUSION

Fathers and mothers have been wired to play specific roles in the upbringing of a child. In today's society, because of certain circumstances, those roles are being challenged, altered, questioned, and even reversed. I believe that fathers seem to conform more comfortably to issues associated with the politics of power, strength, and stability. Mothers, however, do well with issues related to emotion and those issues that keep us grounded in our better qualities as humans. There are no harsh dividing walls between the two, for when it comes to being human, or humane for that matter, we adapt to fulfill the need as it arises. Fathers and mothers should be allowed total access and control over their offspring, except in exceptional cases of neglect and abuse. Families are the foundation of any community or society and are entitled to comprehensive support, not patronage and supervision. If society wants to uphold its moral and social principles, it needs to begin with a firm foundation of strong families who are offered equal opportunities to live up to those principles and aspirations. Society, therefore, needs a proactive system of intervention and support, directed not only to mothers and children, but to fathers as well. There need to be a deliberate and concerted effort to reverse the system of negative publicity and law enforcement being directed against fathers, deadbeat or not. What affects fathers affects their behavior toward their children and their children's response toward them. With most cultures being paternally based, the inconsistencies affecting fathers definitely have an impact on boys, or sons, who become confused, insecure, and stricken with low self-esteem.

This state of mind translates into reactionary behaviors common among those adolescents from broken homes and single-parent families that can go to extremes to get, in an alternative way, the attention they need. These include gang-related crimes, excessive drinking, substance abuse, speeding, and finally, suicides. Girls are equally affected, growing up starved for a male influence and the affection of a father, showing signs of being gutted of their pride and composure, displaying unladylike qualities of behavior and, in some cases, even committing crimes. To correct this catastrophic trend, our approach to families needs to be proactive and holistic, not directed piecemeal to children, girls, and mothers, but to the whole family, including fathers.

When I refer to being versed in the art of love and war, I run the risk of being greatly misunderstood. You can train feverishly day and night your whole life and still not be ready for the next situation in either extreme. Soldiers are brutally prepared for war, and some die before they were even able to raise a finger to use what they had learned. Situations of love and romance are so very unique and problematic, every victim or victor will have to work out his own salvation in the heaven or hell he finds himself. The purpose of the physical training in self-defense is to condition the mind and body in a state of preparedness not to fight and kill indiscriminately because of your superior advantage, but to be able to control your natural impulses and confront the most threatening situation with calm composure and foresight. That is achieved not only by hard, unforgiving, brutal training, but by smart training as well. Training smarter and not harder is the key. You need to focus all your initiatives and your creativity on the shortcuts, the secrets on the essence of any form of attack, so that you can gracefully dance your way past every aggression with little or no effort, demoralizing and frustrating your opponent. Techniques in brutal applications of force are very pedestrian. Although useful at times, they can become addictive and render the mind helpless and demoralized very easily when the opposition gets physically overwhelming. It is the ability to remain calm, focused, calculating, and precise that you will succeed in maneuvering through the tangled web of attacks that come your way. In all conflicts, in circumstances of love and war, it is what registers in the mind of the opponent or lover that is more important than what registers on the body. This is why it is crucial in physical self-defense to acquaint with the different martial arts so that you can decipher the secret of each and induct them into your arsenal to create combinations of your own. You create demons from your imagination, to be your sparring partner in a life-and-death struggle, to test your ideas, reflexes and impulses, and your physical fitness.

Visiting all the annals of erotic arts, from around the world, will not in the least make you more pleasing to a woman. A woman needs to be won, not defeated, and we warriors are wired to fall into the routine of making that fatal mistake. Just, as in self-defense, when you reach a comfortable level of perfection, you become as flexible and adaptable like water to overwhelm and abort your opponent, so in love, you will need to do the same, only this time to soothe and mesmerize in a reciprocal and passive manner so that the victory or the outcome belongs to both of you. Son, you can sweep her off her feet in the dance of love and take over the dance to yourself with her swinging in your arms, until her feet touch the ground, and she will still walk away confused, with a dejected look of dissatisfaction on her face. When I was even in my teens, I wrote for myself the ten commandments of love. As I review them today, I seem to have got it right from the start. Now in my twilight years, I look back with very few regrets. I mean it when I say very few, because all my regrets are based on deliberate decisions I had made based on lack of knowledge, stubbornness, defiance, or downright stupidity which is common among us male species at that age. Out of the bitterness of those regrets came the sweet honey of wisdom I share with you. Remember, however, that they are not yours, but mine, and you cannot learn them from this letter. Wisdom cannot be injected, swallowed, or absorbed into your system. You have to acquire it yourself. May this letter serve as a training of the spirit and the mind so that as you go forward into your life's battles, in love and in war, you will make the decisions and take the right actions, with fewer regrets.

Your loving father.

MAYBE ALONE

Maybe, alone
I can make a start
And pick up the first stone
To move the mountain
And bring some freedom
To humanity
Trapped on the other side of happiness, love, and peace
Maybe, alone
I can turn the tide
With the aqueduct that I build
Against the current of a painful custom
Drifting to a destiny of want, poverty, and dependency
Maybe, alone
I can win the world
To help me
Free it from its travails of ignorance and insensitivity
Maybe, alone.

INDEX

A

adolescence, 31-32, 32-41, 55, 64

B

balance (moderation), 83
Basie, William "Count," 19
battle of illusions, 80-82
betrayal, 85, 95
bipolarism, system of, 14
Brubeck, Dave, 19

C

character, test of man's, 83-84
confidence, 36, 70, 72, 84, 100
conflicts, 39, 61-62, 79, 84, 104
courtship, 47, 63
  entrapments of, 49-50
  partner for, 49-50

rules of, 54-63
strategy in, 49
women and, 105

D

death, 87, 95
defense
  aspects of, 68
  personal, 69
demons, 65, 79, 88
  nature of, 81-82
  potential, 82-83
discipline, intrinsic, 20

E

education, 32-33, 42-44
  functional, 37-38
Ellington, Duke, 19
emotions, 50-51, 58

Edwards Brothers, Inc.
Thorofare, NJ USA
November 1, 2011